ADVANCE PRAISE FOR
"I've Always Been a Yankees Fan"

"Hillary thinks that nobody is keeping track and that her quotes will never catch up with her. But Thomas Kuiper did keep track. This wonderful little book will...make sure that Hillary's quotes and lies are not forgotten but come back to haunt her."

—Dick Morris, author, *Condi vs. Hillary*,
(from the Foreword)

"I've Always Been a Yankees Fan *is a great collection of Hillary Clinton's own statements that leaves no doubt as to what she is really like. This could be Hillary's* Unfit for Command."
—Joe Klein, author, *Global Deception: The UN's Stealth Assault on America's Freedom*

"No one can describe Hillary like Hillary. I've Always Been a Yankees Fan *is brilliant for letting Hillary Clinton speak for herself, and I have no doubt that the American people will be very interested in what she has to say."*

—Lucianne Goldberg, publisher, Lucianne.com News Forum

"Hillary Clinton's own words reveal her as a ruthless, crass, and power-hungry politician. Thomas Kuiper has done the world a service by shining a spotlight on the true nature of this woman who wants to be president."

—Candice E. Jackson, author, *Their Lives: The Women Targeted by the Clinton Machine*

"I'VE ALWAYS BEEN A YANKEES FAN"

"I'VE ALWAYS BEEN A YANKEES FAN"

HILLARY CLINTON IN HER OWN WORDS

THOMAS D. KUIPER

World Ahead Publishing, Inc.

Published by World Ahead Publishing, Inc., Los Angeles, CA

World Ahead Publishing's books are available at special discounts for bulk purchases. For more information, visit www.worldahead.com.

First Edition

ISBN 0-9746701-8-9
LCCN 2006921129

Printed in the United States of America

Dedicated to
Barbara Olson and Michael Kelly,
two patriots tragically lost
in the War on Terror

TABLE OF CONTENTS

Foreword

SOMETIMES a politician is her own worst enemy. That's the case with Hillary Rodham Clinton. She often speaks without thinking and impulsively misrepresents the truth. She said she was named after Sir Edmund Hillary, who climbed Mt. Everest. The problem is that he climbed the mountain years after she was born. She said she always rooted for the New York Yankees when she decided to run for the Senate in New York, but during the Democratic Convention in Chicago in 1996, she said she was a Chicago Cubs fan, as a native of that city.

Hillary thinks that nobody is keeping track and that her quotes will never catch up with her. But Thomas Kuiper did keep track. He went through all the records and the clips and the files. The result is this book.

It's worth buying and reading for its entertainment value alone. No politician could possibly amass quotes like this and expect to run for public office. Nobody would dare.

But it has an importance that goes beyond human interest and humor. This woman wants to be president of the United States. She will run in 2008. You need this book in self-defense, so that you can fight to save our country from her presidency. She is one of the most ruthless people we have ever seen in politics and she doesn't belong in the White House—at either end of the building, the president's office or the residence.

This wonderful little book will give you all the ammunition you need to hold up your end of the argument and make sure that Hillary's quotes and lies are not forgotten but come back to haunt her.

Dick Morris, author, *Condi vs. Hillary*

Acknowledgments

THANK YOU to Ami Naramor, Eric Jackson, Norman Book, Judy Abarbanel, and everyone at World Ahead Publishing.

To Anna G. Folmer, Hena Cuevas, Marisa C. Casa, Patrick "Mr. Liberal" Hanavan, and Peter Mallari. Thank you for your friendship and moral support throughout the long process of finally getting published.

Thank you to Chris Ruddy, and all the people at Newsmax.

Special thanks to Dick Morris, for his generous participation in this project.

My siblings; Rich, Cathy, Liz, & James, have been of great moral support. As have both of my "liberal" parents. My mother, Roberta "I can't believe all my children are Republicans" Snow; and father, Doug "I hate that Rush Limbaugh" Kuiper.

Finally, a sincere and special thank you to Senator Hillary Rodham Clinton. Were it not for your expressive nature, and lack of sound judgment, this book would not have been possible.

Style & Credits

ALL OUTSIDE works referenced within the text of *I've Always Been a Yankees Fan* are cited according to book title, newspaper or magazine title, or website name. When applicable, the name of the article author or article title referred to has been included in the text before the parenthetical citation. I have chosen not to follow the *Chicago Manual of Style* in the text as many of the books cited are best-sellers and are easily recognizable. For more complete bibliographic information, please refer to the "References" section, at the back of the book.

All photographs included in *I've Always Been a Yankees Fan*, unless otherwise indicated in the text, are reprinted courtesy of AP/WideWorld Photos.

**What I would like in an ideal world,
is for people to get to know Hillary.**

*Lisa Caputo, former press secretary to Hillary Clinton
(TheNewAmerican.com, 07/12/93)*

CHAPTER ONE:
Hillary the Patriot

Land that I Love

Where is the goddamn fucking flag?...I want the goddamn fucking flag up every fucking morning at fucking sunrise.

Anxious to honor America, Hillary said this to the staff at the Arkansas governor's mansion on Labor Day, 1991 (Inside the White House, p. 244).

I pledge allegiance to the America that can be.

Hillary was reluctant to say the Pledge of Allegiance, according to pundit Chris Matthews, so she used this wording instead (The Tim Russert Show, 11/24/01). *This caused Mr. Matthews to ask, "What are we, on probation?"* (Newsmax.com, 02/27/02).

Extremists fail to provide a viable pathway from the Cold War to the global village.

Criticizing those in favor of limited government (You Don't Say, pp. 23-24). *In Hillary's world, Conservative = Extremist.*

The picture of patriotism.

To Serve and Protect

Fuck off! It's enough that I have to see you shit-kickers every day. I'm not going to talk to you, too. Just do your goddamn job and keep your mouth shut.

To her state trooper bodyguards, after one of them greeted her with "good morning" (American Evita, p. 90). *Some of these same troopers later considered going public during the 1992 presidential campaign with their knowledge of Governor Clinton's womanizing. However, they were warned by Clinton's*

people, "If you know what's good for you, you'll keep your mouth shut" (Blood Sport, *p. 320).*

[You] fucking idiot.

Hillary to a state trooper who was driving her to an event (Crossfire, *p. 84). Former trooper Larry Gleghorn said of Hillary: "She was a bitch day in and day out. She always screamed we were taking her the wrong route when we drove her to an event"* (The First Partner, *p. 119).*

[We] have nothing but praise for their courage, integrity, and professionalism, and we feel lucky to remain friends with many agents who protected us.

Hillary's characterization of the Clintons' relationship with the Secret Service agents responsible for their protection (Living History, *p. 131).*

One of the "personal, trained pigs," helping Hillary down the stairs.

Personal, trained pigs.

An apparently common designation the Clintons used for their security details that reveals a somewhat different view of the Secret Service (Unlimited Access, *p. 90). According to Gary Aldrich, "[Hillary] had a clear dislike for the agents, bordering on hatred...Two Secret Service agents heard Hillary's daughter Chelsea refer to them as 'personal, trained pigs'...The agent on the detail tried to scold Chelsea for such disrespect. He told her...he believed that her father, the president, would be shocked if he heard what she had just said to her friends. Chelsea's response? 'I don't think so. That's what my parents call you'"* (Unlimited Access, *p. 90).*

[The Secret Service] will shut down the entire Eastern Seaboard just to embarrass us if we give them the excuse...They do this to us all the time. They're mainly Republicans. They hate us. They always take the most extreme option just to cause us embarrassment.

Another revealing comment of Hillary's about the Secret Service (Rewriting History, *p. 137*). *Note:* Webster's Dictionary *defines paranoia as a "disorder marked by delusions of persecution or of grandeur."*

If you want to remain on this detail, get your fucking ass over here and grab those bags.

Hillary's order to a Secret Service agent who was reluctant to carry her luggage because he wanted to keep his hands free in case of an incident (The First Partner, *p. 259*). *Years later, Chris Matthews said he witnessed Senator Clinton using a member of her Secret Service unit to carry her luggage on the Washington to New York shuttle. "Who in the Senate gets a sherpa to carry their bags for them? Who pays the airfare for this guy? Who pays for his lifestyle? Who pays his salary to walk around carrying her bags? This looks pretty regal"* (Hardball, *08/01, quoted on* Newsmax.com, *07/17/01*).

Get fucked! Get the fuck out of my way! Get out of my face!

Various comments that Hillary's Secret Service detail heard from her (Hillary's Scheme, *p. 89*). Family Circle *once wrote of Hillary, "In many ways, you couldn't ask for a more 'traditional' First Lady"* (TheNewAmerican.com, *07/12/93*).

Stay the fuck back, stay the fuck away from me! Don't come within ten yards of me, or else!...Just fucking do as I say, okay?

More pleasantries from the first lady to the Secret Service detail in charge of protecting her life (Unlimited Access, *p. 139*). *Ronald Kessler wrote in* A Matter of Character (*p. 2*), *"Secret Service agents assigned at various points to guard Hillary during her campaign for the Senate were dismayed at how two-faced and unbalanced she was."*

What the fuck is going on?

To a Secret Service agent after Hillary read an article, written by a UC Berkeley student, critical of Stanford's newest high-profile undergrad, Chelsea Clinton (SFGate.com, 11/26/97). The student was later interrogated by the Secret Service, by order of Mrs. Clinton (SFGate.com, 11/26/97).

Not All That They Could Be

Well—but if you look at the platform of the Democratic Party, we take a very tough stance on national defense.

(Meet The Press, *08/29/04).*

Put this on the ground! I left my sunglasses in the limo. I need those sunglasses. We need to go back!

Ordering the presidential helicopter, Marine One, to turn back while en route to Air Force One (Dereliction of Duty, *pp. 71-72).*

A typical Democratic "tough stance" on national defense.

Senator Clinton pictured with one of her "supporters" while visiting Iraq. This serviceman later stated that he was ordered to have his picture taken with Hillary, which was why he was giving the sign of coercion (TruthorFiction.com, 05/02/05).

I have been always trying to figure where that [story about banning military uniforms in the White House] got started...but I certainly had nothing to do with it, and I know my husband didn't.

Denying that she was anti-military while first lady (The Brian Lehrer Show, 12/08/03). According to Lt. Col. Robert "Buzz" Patterson, the directive banning military uniforms did come from Hillary through Leon Panetta: "It's ridiculous for her to claim that the story was the result of some young staffer who...said something critical to someone in uniform. It was all Hillary's doing from beginning to end" (The Truth About Hillary, pp. 230-231).

I knew that Bill respected military service, that he would have served had he been called...

Writing about the controversy over Clinton dodging the draft during the Vietnam War (Living History, p. 240). Oddly enough, Hillary neglected to mention Bill's famous letter from 1969 where he wrote that he "loath[ed] the military" (Congressional Record, H5550, 07/30/93).

Bill, this is you! I can hear you saying this.

Hillary upon realizing the authenticity of the same 1969 letter of Bill Clinton's, where Clinton also thanked ROTC officer Colonel Holmes for "saving me from the draft" (All Too Human, *p. 75).*

No matter what you think about the Iraq war, there is one thing we can all agree on for the next days—we have to salute the courage and bravery of those who are risking their lives to vote and those brave Iraqi and American soldiers fighting to protect their right to vote.

Hillary's public opinion of the people voting in the Iraqi elections and the soldiers protecting them (Clinton.Senate.gov, 01/28/05).

CHAPTER TWO:
"Eighteen Wonderful Years"

I (Heart) Arkansas

I followed my heart and went to Arkansas.

Hillary's explanation for her move from Washington, D.C. in 1974 to be with Bill, just after the completion of Watergate (Newsmax.com, 06/09/03).

I've got to be there just to make sure they don't fuck it up.

The explanation Hillary gave a colleague as to why she went to Arkansas to work on Bill's campaign for Congress (American Evita, pp. 52-53).

My parents didn't even know where Arkansas was...They thought I'd end up in Washington, D.C. doing something with my life.

Circa 1976, recounting her parents' disappointment about her being a politician's wife from a small, southern state (Blood Sport, p. 57). By most measures, Arkansas ranks forty-ninth among the fifty states, which is why the state's unofficial motto is "Thank God for Mississippi." However, since Hillary's parents did not go to school in Arkansas, they should have been able to find it on a map.

A bespectacled Hillary picks out her future office during a White House visit in the 1980s.

I think Arkansas is a wonderful place and filled with some of the best people I've ever been privileged to know or work with.

(The Unique Voice of Hillary Rodham Clinton, p. 17). *Hillary once told one of her Arkansas bodyguards to keep his mouth shut when they were traveling out of state because "you sound like a hick"* (American Evita, p. 90).

One of the "colorful people," Susan McDougal, looking very stylish in this orange ensemble.

Before I moved to Little Rock, I had spent a lifetime dealing with David Kendall-type[s]... I thought it would be nice to deal with the colorful people of Arkansas for a change.

Regarding people such as Jim and Susan Mc-Dougal and other Arkansans involved in the Whitewater investigation (The Seduction of Hillary, p. 404).

We Arkansans have to quit making excuses and accept...the challenge of excellence.

A speech to her "fellow Arkansans" (On The Make, p. 285).

The state of Arkansas is a place that has...just so much to be proud of.

More glowing words for her adopted home state (The New York Times, 04/23/94).

Bimbos, sluts, trailer trash, rednecks, and shit-kickers.

Common terms that Hillary used to describe her fellow Arkansans (American Evita, p. 139). *In a February 2005 interview, New York congressman Charles Rangel said of Hillary's decision to follow Bill to Arkansas, "That's a hell of a move to make for a redneck"* (Newsmax.com, 02/15/05).

The people were warm and welcoming to me. I felt very much at home.

Reflecting on her move to Arkansas to join her boyfriend Bill Clinton in 1974 (Newsweek, 03/30/92). Senator Clinton, D-NY, would also later state she spent "eighteen wonderful years" in Arkansas.

When I look at what's available in the man department [in Arkansas], I'm surprised more women aren't gay.

To female friends about the lack of quality men (Bill & Hillary, p. 173).

Wooooooooooo, Pig! Sooie!

Goddamn L.D., did you see that family right out of *Deliverance*? Get me the hell out of here!

To her bodyguard, L.D. Brown, after meeting some of the "colorful people" at a county fair in northern Arkansas in the early 1980s (Crossfire, p. 85). In her autobiography, Hillary writes that she "always liked campaigning and traveling in Arkansas, stopping at country stores, sale barns, and barbecue joints" (Living History, p. 93).

I had never before lived in a place so small, friendly, and Southern, and I loved it. I went to Arkansas Razorbacks football games and learned to call the hogs.

(Living History, p. 71).

This is the kind of shit I have to put up with.

Her remarks to a friend after a Clinton supporter gave her a pair of earrings shaped like Arkansas Razorbacks (Blood Sport, p. 105).

Jesus, Bill, I know you've got all these redneck relatives...But the Klan?

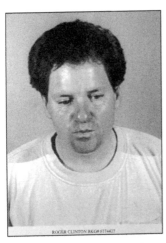

ROGER CLINTON BKG# 6774427

Redneck Relative—Exhibit A.

Confronting her Arkansas-native husband when she discovered that one of his long-lost relatives was a member of the KKK, circa 1993 (Bill & Hillary, p. 273). This concern for racial issues apparently did not extend past those that impacted her political future, however, as Hillary vigorously opposed President Bush's appointment of Charles Pickering—a man who fought tirelessly against the Klan in his home state of Mississippi in the 1960s—to the federal bench. (Clinton.Senate.gov, 01/16/04).

I suspect people will be getting tired of hearing from Mrs. Bill Clinton.

To the press in the early stages of Bill's 1982 campaign for governor, stating that she no longer would be known as Hillary Rodham, but instead as Hillary Clinton or Mrs. Bill Clinton (First In His Class, p. 400). At this same press conference, Hillary had to confess that she had not legally changed her name to Hillary Clinton or registered to vote by this name.

We shouldn't lose the election over this issue.

Hillary agreeing to change her name from Rodham to Clinton in preparation for Bill's 1982 race for governor of Arkansas. She had just received polling information that revealed many voters disliked the fact she never took her husband's name (Hell To Pay, p. 190).

We shouldn't run the risk. What if it's one percent of the vote? What if it's two percent?

More principled reasoning from Hillary as to why she should change her name from Rodham to Clinton (First In His Class, p. 399).

It was a personal decision, but it was prompted by political considerations.

Explaining why she finally took her husband's name, seven years after they were married (Primetime, 01/30/92). *A former friend of Hillary's later recounted a different reason for the name change: "The deal was, she gave up her name and her integrity in exchange for his promise to take them where she wanted to go—to be president together"* (Hillary's Choice, *p. 146*).

Life with Governor Bill Clinton

For God's sake Bill, don't be an asshole. If you want to lose this election because you're too chickenshit, then go ahead!

Hillary speaking from her heart to cherished husband and candidate Bill Clinton regarding campaign tactics in Arkansas (Bill & Hillary, *p. 145*).

Motherfucker, Cocksucker.

Some of Hillary's more choice names for her husband (Boy Clinton, *p. 278*).

Shit, Bill, even Nixon wasn't that stupid.

Chastising her husband when she discovered he offered federal jobs to Arkansas troopers to buy their silence about his womanizing while governor (American Evita, *p. 136*).

Now, Bill. Now.

Urging her husband in 1988 to run for president (Bill & Hillary, *p. 217*).

I want to go to supper with my husband, I want to go the movies. I want to go on vacation with my family. I want my husband back.

To the Arkansas press, explaining how happy she was when Bill decided not to run for president in 1988 (Bill & Hillary, *pp. 221-222*). *According to Christopher Andersen, the real reason Clinton did not run that year was that mem-*

bers of his staff advised against it, knowing his reckless womanizing would prove too damaging. A few years earlier, Hillary had hired a private detective to verify her suspicions of Bill's philandering (Bill & Hillary, p. 220).

He only does that to people he loves.

To Dick Morris, circa 1990, after Bill Clinton physically assaulted him, because Morris was quitting his campaign (Shadow, p. 332). *In an article entitled "Setting the Record Straight," Morris later wrote that when this story threatened to surface during the 1992 presidential campaign, Hillary instructed him to "say it never happened"* (National Review Online, 06/12/03).

Part of growing up is learning to control one's impulses, which is often difficult for young people.

Lecturing teens on the value of abstinence (Guardian Unlimited, 04/27/99).

As the designers of this German float noted, controlling one's impulses can sometimes be difficult for presidents, too.

He is an incredibly loving and compassionate and caring person.

Her response when asked about Bill's character (The First Partner, *p. 211).*

[You] goddamn stupid fucking fool.

To Bill, in front of toddler Chelsea (Newsmax.com, 07/15/00).

A psychologist once told me that for a boy, being in the middle of a conflict between two women is the worst possible situation. There is always the desire to please each one.

Rationalizing Clinton's womanizing by explaining that young Bill Clinton was caught between his mother and aunt, who were always fighting (The Final Days, *p. 105).*

Bill and I have always loved each other...I'm proud of my marriage.

(The Unique Voice of Hillary Rodham Clinton, *p. 48). According to Ivan Duda, the private detective hired by Hillary to look into Bill's womanizing, "Her purpose in having me find out about these women was not so she could confront Bill with the hurt attitude...Instead, it was damage control, pure and simple"* (Bill & Hillary, *p. 185).*

CHAPTER THREE:
The Co-Presidency

The 1992 Election—Destiny Calls Us

I never thought that the long-haired, bearded boy I married in law school would end up being president. I don't think like that.

To Katie Couric in 2004 (The Today Show, 04/16/04).

He's going to be president of the United States.

Hillary, as a Watergate staff attorney in 1974, bragging to co-worker Bernie Nussbaum about her boyfriend, Bill Clinton (Partners in Power, p. 166).

I want you to do damage control over Bill's philandering...Bill's going to be president of the United States...I want you to get rid of all these bitches he's seeing...I want you to give me the names and addresses and phone numbers, and we can get them under control.

Hillary's instructions to private detective Ivan Duda in the 1980s, when Bill's womanizing was at its peak (The Truth About Hillary, pp. 98-99).

If I didn't kick his ass every morning, he'd never amount to anything.

To a friend regarding Bill (Hillary's Choice, p. 136).

Hillary displaying one of her better "ass kicking" stares.

Hillary on the Campaign Trail

I feel very comfortable about my husband and about our marriage.

During the 1992 campaign, addressing all those "false" rumors about her husband being a womanizer (Newsweek, 02/03/92). It was during this period that the Gennifer Flowers accusations first appeared. Even though Bill later confirmed he had an affair with Gennifer, Hillary still refers to Flowers' story as "a whale of a tale" in her autobiography (Living History, p. 106).

I suppose I could've stayed home and baked cookies and had teas...

Her reaction to being criticized by Jerry Brown during the 1992 primaries for her questionable ethics and business transactions during the 1980s, or "Reagan's decade of greed" (Nightline, 03/26/92). She's often used the "I'm only being criticized because I'm a woman" defense. She said at this time, "this is the kind of thing that happens to...women who have their own careers and their own lives...but I guess it's something that we're [she and her fellow liberated women] going to have to live with" (Living History, p. 109).

Just the kind of headline that would make any woman "comfortable" about her marriage.

I've made my share of cookies and served hundreds of cups of tea...so it never occurred to me that my comment would be taken as insulting mothers.

Hillary in top CYA form after her "cookies and tea" comment didn't sit well with voters (The Unique Voice of Hillary Rodham Clinton, *p. 46*).

Besides, I've done quite a lot of cookie-baking in my day, and tea-pouring, too.

(Living History, *p. 109*). *During the 1992 campaign, Hillary and Barbara Bush took part in a cookie-baking contest, with Hillary prevailing. It was later disclosed that a friend actually baked Hillary's cookies.*

I'm not sitting here like some little woman standing by her man like Tammy Wynette. I'm sitting here because I love him and I honor what he's been through and what we've been through together.

A famous zinger from the 1992 campaign (60 Minutes, *01/26/92*). *During the same interview, Hillary blamed the claims of Ms. Flowers and other women of having affairs with her husband on—who else—Republicans, saying, "I felt terrible about what was happening...she said sort of wacky things, which we thought were attributable to the fact she was terrified."*

I didn't mean to hurt Tammy Wynette...I happen to be a country-western fan.

Hillary apologizing for her Tammy Wynette comment so as not to alienate country-music lovers or their "shit-kicking" cousins (Bill & Hillary, *p. 236*).

[I'll do] whatever it takes to get us elected.

Evincing even less than the usual measure of scruples for a politician, Hillary indicates the degree to which she is willing to go to get Bill elected president (Bill & Hillary, *p. 247*).

If you vote for my husband, you get me. It's a two-for-one blue plate special.

Another famous quote from the 1992 campaign (Bill & Hillary, *p. 233*).

[R]emaking of the American way of politics, government, indeed, life...I have a burning desire to do what I can.

Hillary states her goals in the upcoming Clinton administration, during the 1992 campaign (The Seduction of Hillary Rodham, p. 291).

Although I'm not a big fan of it, we might have to move towards an ID system, even for citizens.

Senator Clinton speculating about further ways to remake the American way of life (The Washington Times, 12/13/04).

Inauguration Day

Goddamn it, Bill, you promised me that office!

The infamous Inauguration Day fight regarding whether or not Hillary would receive an office in the West Wing (Bill & Hillary, p. 258). Hillary was furious because Bill had reneged on his promise, part of their power-sharing agreement, to give her the office that traditionally goes to the vice president.

The co-presidents being sworn into office.

You fucking asshole!

More encouraging words from Hillary on Inauguration Day to the newly sworn-in Bill Clinton (Hillary's Choice, p. 223). *President Clinton once opined, "...if everybody in this country had the character that my wife has, [it would] be a better place to live"* (Absolute Power, p. 85).

You stupid motherfucker!

A final Inauguration Day salvo directed at the President (The Seduction of Hillary Rodham, p. 321). *Hillary wrote in her autobiography, "Bill Clinton and I started a conversation in the spring of 1971, and more than thirty years later we're still talking"*(Living History, p. 75).

Hillarycare

Gentlemen, I have looked at your proposal, and it's pure bullshit! Now, you've had your meeting! Get out!

Hillary's only words when she met with health insurance executives who had a proposal for health care reform, circa 1993 (Unlimited Access, p. 88).

I'm sure you will do that, Mr. Armey...You and Dr. Kevorkian.

Testifying before Congress in 1993, Hillary snaps at Representative Dick Armey, R-TX, because he previously had the gall to criticize her health care plan, saying it was one that Dr. Kevorkian would have loved (Larry King Live, 01/06/01).

We have been left on the medical and scientific sidelines.

Hillary spewing the tired feminist rant that only 13 percent of federal medical research dollars go to study female health problems (The Hillary Trap, p. 20). *Hillary failed to mention that only 7 percent go toward men's health problems, with the remaining 80 percent going to study diseases affecting both sexes.*

We just can't trust the American people to make those types of choices... Government has to make those choices for people.

Hillary to Representative Dennis Hastert, R-Ill, on the issue of who should control the allocation of money in her health care reform plan, circa June 1993 (The Seduction of Hillary Rodham, *p. 334*). *Hastert wrote of this discussion: "As Hillary Clinton once told me...people are basically greedy and won't make the tough decisions. They won't take their kid to the hospital when he needs to go because they want to keep the money for themselves"* (Speaker, *p. 249*).

We can't afford to have that money go to the private sector. The money has to go to the federal government because the federal government will spend that money better than the private sector will spend it.

More to Dennis Hastert regarding health care reform (The Seduction of Hillary Rodham, *p. 334*).

[Insurance companies] like being able to exclude people from coverage because the more they can exclude, the more money they can make.

(The New York Times, *11/02/93*).

I said they were purchasing cooperatives and that's what they're going to be!

An angry Hillary responding to concerns that her plan to have "purchasing cooperatives" sounded too much like regulatory agencies (The Survivor, *p. 116*). *Members of the Clinton economic team also had concerns about her plan. However, Hillary "seemed uninterested in, or even hostile to, their advice, so they soon learned to stop giving it"* (The Survivor, *p. 116*).

That's the truth and they'd better get used to it.

Circa 1993, Hillary regarding the $100 billion price tag of health care reform, which many felt would cripple small businesses (The Agenda, *p. 169*).

When these guys see the people out there demanding reform then they'll get off their asses and do something about it.

Expressing confidence that Congress would pass her health care plan (American Evita, p. 142).

We were on the front lines of an increasingly hostile ideological conflict between centrist Democrats and a Republican Party that was swinging further and further to the right.

A self-righteous Hillary rationalizing the defeat of her health care reform plan (Living History, p. 230). Just months after her "reform" was declared DOA, the American people returned control of Congress to the party "that was swinging further and further to the right."

Contrary to the snappy slogan, Hillarycare would soon disappear, taking Democratic control of Congress with it.

Now, you may remember, I had a few ideas about health care, and I've learned a few lessons since then, but I haven't given up on the goal, and that's why we kept working step-by-step to insure millions of children through the Children's Health Insurance Program.

A speech at the 2000 Democratic National Convention (USAToday.com, 08/15/00). Some of her ideas regarding health care reform led to her task force being sued. U.S. District Court Judge Royce Lamberth ruled that members of Hillary's task force "intended to deceive the court" when they gave sworn testimony. He went on to state, "The Executive Branch of the government…was dishonest with this court, and the government must now face the consequences…It seems that some government officials never learn that the cover up can be worse than the underlying conduct" (The New York Times, 12/19/97).

"I'm Not Really Governing"

It's been exhilarating, frustrating, eye opening…Just to set the record straight, I'm not really governing.

Hillary's response to Bill Moyers's question, "What's it like to govern the country?" early in the Clintons' first term (TheNewAmerican.com, 07/12/93). Upon hearing Hillary's denial that she was in charge, then-Texas Governor Ann Richards said, "If you believe that, I've got a bridge I'd like to show you" (TheNewAmerican.com, 07/12/93).

How could you be so damn stupid? How could you do that?

To President Clinton, early in the first term in front of guests at the White House, after he did something of which she disapproved (U.S. News & World Report, 02/05/96).

As a general proposition, high-ranking government officials are not subject to depositions.

Hillary Clinton attempting to avoid a deposition by making the novel argument that she, as first lady, was a senior government official of the executive branch, and therefore not subject to the normal court regulations (Judicial Watch Press Release, 07/15/99).

I'm not going to have some reporters pawing through our papers. We are the president.

Regarding the subpoenaed Whitewater documents that the press wanted access to (BrainyQuotes.com, 01/22/06).

Bill and I didn't come to Washington to do business as usual and compromise.

Hillary refusing to discuss a compromise with the Republicans over her health care reform plan, circa 1993 ("The Clinton Years," Frontline, 01/30/96). Around that time, Bill Clinton said, "We can't be so fixated on our desire to preserve the rights of ordinary Americans..." (USA Today, 03/11/93).

What the fuck are you doing up there? You get back here right away.

Chastising President Clinton over the phone after she learned he floated a proposal for health care reform that differed from her plan of 100 percent coverage for all citizens (The Survivor, p. 118). The next day Clinton retracted his proposal and stated that he was committed to 100 percent coverage.

Come back here, you asshole! Where the fuck do you think you're going?

To Bill as he tried to avoid her after an article appeared in the newspaper that angered her (Unlimited Access, p. 192). Former Clinton advisor David Gergen wrote of the marriage, "A chipper president would arrive at the office in the morning, almost whistling as he whipped through papers. A phone would ring. It was a call from upstairs at the residence...his mood would darken, his attention wander, and hot words would spew out...What, I would wonder, had she said to him now?" (Eyewitness to Power, p. 274).

From my perspective, our marriage is a strong marriage. We love each other.

(The Unique Voice of Hillary Rodham Clinton, *p. 49). According to Ronald Kessler, "As in the movie* Dave, *Bill and Hillary would emerge from the marine helicopter holding hands. But once inside the White House [out of public view] they would start screaming at each other, and Bill would slink off to have phone sex with Monica Lewinsky"* (A Matter of Character, *p. 116).*

We talk about everything, and have for as long as we've known each other…particularly on issues where we share a common commitment.

(The Case Against Hillary Clinton, *p. 22). However, when she was asked about whether they discussed pardoning the FALN (Armed Forces of National Liberation) terrorists, Hillary said, "I don't talk about what I talked to the president about on any issue"* (CBSNews.com, *03/14/00).*

I'm just so confused, I don't know what works anymore. I don't trust my own judgment.

Remarks to Dick Morris after the 1994 midterm election where the Republicans gained control of Congress for the first time in forty years (Hillary's Choice, *p. 253). Most political pundits stated the main reason for the Republicans' victory was the Clinton administration's arrogance and raging ineptitude during its first two years in office, especially the handling of the health care reform plan, which was Hillary's project.*

I don't know how to handle this. Everything I do seems not to work. Nothing goes right. I just don't know what to do.

More to Dick Morris (Hillary's Choice, *p. 253).*

Remind me, have I ever done anything right in my life?

Circa November 1994, after the Republicans take control of Congress, Hillary has a moment of self-pity (Newsweek, *01/15/96). In October of 1994, her 1,342-page health care reform plan died a dismal death in Congress.*

We came here to do good things, and we just didn't understand so many things about this town. It's been so hard.

To Clinton advisor David Gergen after she ignored his advice about being more cooperative towards the press (Eyewitness To Power, p. 299). Many of the failures and problems of the Clintons' first term—Whitewater, the failed nominees for attorney general, Travelgate, Filegate, cattle futures, and the failure of healthcare—all had Hillary's fingerprints on them. In 1995, she took a much lower profile in the Clinton administration. About the same time, she allegedly began having conversations with the ghost of Eleanor Roosevelt.

I've been a part of it, part of the administration, and I've worked on a lot of issues...and part of what I bring to this race is an understanding and involvement in the working of this administration.

Hillary "I'm not really governing" Clinton commenting on her experience in the Clinton administration, and how it will help make her a better senator (NewsMax.com, 07/10/00).

I know a little bit about what it's like on the other end of Pennsylvania Avenue making these difficult decisions.

Hillary Clinton to Tim Russert regarding supporting President Bush in the War on Terror (Meet The Press, 09/15/02).

Why can't anybody understand that I truly love this man?

In a phone call to Dick Morris (Rewriting History, p. 195). Regarding the Clintons' marriage, Morris has said on numerous occasions, "Hillary loves Bill. And Bill loves Bill. It gives them something in common."

CHAPTER FOUR:
"The Most Ethical Administration"

Whitewater

If Reaganomics works at all, Whitewater could become the Western Hemisphere's Mecca.

Hillary to Jim McDougal regarding her excitement over her investment in the new project called Whitewater (Blood Sport, *p. 100*).

JFK had real men in his White House!

Taunting her husband's aides for being wimps because they didn't fight hard enough to oppose the Whitewater investigation (The Survivor, *p. 108*).

George Stephanopoulos, inadvertently proving Hillary's point.

No! Jim told me that this was going to pay for college for Chelsea. I still expect it to do that!

HRC's response to Susan and Jim McDougal's offer to buy the Clintons out of the Whitewater deal—the McDougals were concerned about a possible future scandal for the Clintons, circa 1985 (Blood Sport, p. 133).

Goddamn it...You bastard...It's your fucking fault.

To President Clinton, after receiving some bad news regarding the Whitewater investigation (Dereliction of Duty, p. 68). The same author also wrote, "I witnessed several incidents like this; and while I got used to Hillary's wrath, her ability to turn it off and on amazed me" (Dereliction of Duty, p. 68).

I really like it when Jim goes in to see Bill because it makes him feel good.

Regarding Jim McDougal's regular visits (Arkansas Mischief, p. 157).

The unstable liar going to prison to protect Hillary.

She is such a liar...She's crazy, unstable, and totally dishonest. You can't trust a thing she says.

Fuming to Dick Morris, when it appeared that Susan McDougal would testify against the Clintons (Rewriting History, p. 159).

I feel very confident about how this will all turn out. This is not a long-term problem or issue in any way.

During the April 1994 "pretty in pink" press conference, Hillary's prediction of the recently undertaken Whitewater investigation (Shadow, p. 253). The Whitewater investigation would later result in the conviction and sentencing of Bill's successor, Arkansas Governor

Jim Guy Tucker, as well as time in jail for both Jim and Susan McDougal. The investigation would not be formally concluded until 2001, and the Clintons finally paid off their legal bills in 2005.

We own half of it, and we are not getting out of it. It's incredible that partners would be asked to sign over their stock.

Hillary's response to Susan McDougal's request of her to rescind power-of-attorney for Whitewater, circa 1992 (Blood Sport, p. 222).

If we did something improper, then how come we lost money?

Explaining why the Clintons supposedly lost almost $69,000 in the Whitewater deal (American Evita, p. 112). Had the Clintons really lost any money in Whitewater, they were legally entitled to deduct the amount on their income taxes. Their taxes show no deductions during the years in question. During this period Hillary was, however, deduction-obsessed enough to deduct Bill's used underwear, which was given to the Salvation Army.

Castle Grande was a trailer park on a piece of property that was about a thousand acres big. I never did any work on Castle Grande.

Denying her involvement in Whitewater to Barbara Walters (20/20, 01/19/96). Charles Peacock, one of Bill Clinton's Arkansas supporters, who was involved in the Whitewater deal and was the former director of the Arkansas Savings and Loan Association, explained why he lied about a campaign contribution to Clinton in the following manner: "I'm a politician, and as a politician I have the prerogative to lie whenever I want" (Inside the White House, p. 235).

The billing records show I did not do work for Castle Grande. I did work for something called IDC, which was not related to Castle Grande.

To Barbara Walters, explaining she knew the Whitewater project by a different name (20/20, 01/19/96). This denial by Hillary prompted Susan McDougal to state, "It was always the same thing. As far as I know, IDC and Castle Grande were one and the same" ("The Clinton Years," Frontline, 01/30/96).

The problem back then, you'll remember, is that documents were destroyed, tapes were missing 18 and a half minutes. The White House was not cooperating...I think the contrast is so dramatic.

Hillary explains why the Clinton White House was innocent of wrongdoing in its various scandals, while the Nixon White House was so dramatically different (The Washington Post, 01/11/96). *In a further example of irony, Monica Lewinsky lived at the Watergate.*

The Missing Files

There was a very bright, young attorney in our law firm who had a relationship with one of the officers of Madison. [He] did all the work.

Hillary denying any substantial involvement in Whitewater, circa April 1994 (The Wall Street Journal, 01/05/96). *When the Rose Law Firm billing records reappeared in 1996, they verify that HRC spent over sixty billable hours working on Whitewater matters. At the time of the deal, savings and loan employee Don Denton tried to warn her that the agreement she was drafting for Whitewater was an illegal transaction. She dismissed his warning by saying, in effect, "You take care of the S&L, and I'll take care of the legal aspects"* (Frontline, 10/07/97).

Every document that we have obtained has been turned over to the special counsel.

Hillary regarding missing Whitewater documents (Blood Sport, p. 24). *She also said of Whitewater, "We know we lost money. We lost a bunch of money for us. Goodness knows what you all would be saying if we made any money. I'm glad we lost money"* (The New York Times, 03/15/94).

We actually did that with *The New York Times*. We took every document we had—which again, I have to say, were not many—we laid them all out.

Hillary, while on The Diane Rehm Show, *claiming to have been completely forthcoming in producing all the Whitewater documents to the media (Shadow, p. 309). Her aides later had to admit to* The New York Times *that she was "mistaken." They purposely did not produce every document they possessed about Whitewater to the press. In fact, the Clinton White House had developed a confrontational approach in dealing with Jeff Gerth, the main writer from the* Times *working on Whitewater stories. This approach became known as the "Fuck you, Jeff Gerth" strategy (Hillary's Choice, p. 206).*

There would be no reason for anyone I know, including myself, not to have wanted them to come out years ago. Why on earth would I not want them out? I would have published them in the paper if I had known.

Explaining to Harry Smith how happy she was that the billing records were finally found (CBS Morning News, 01/19/96).

Some of Hillary's fellow citizens making a statement about the
trustworthiness of her Whitewater testimony.

Oh, that didn't happen, and I know nothing about any other such stories…Absolutely not.

Hillary doing her best Sgt. Schultz imitation during the 1994 "pretty in pink" press conference about the shredding of Whitewater documents at the Rose Law firm (Nightline, 01/30/96). Years later on a different subject, Senator Clinton said, "I am particularly horrified by the use of propaganda and the manipulation of the truth and the revision of history" (CNN.com, 03/31/99).

Because of our experience with the Nixon impeachment in 1974, Bernie [Nussbaum] and I believed that we should cooperate fully with the government investigation….

Explaining that she and the White House counsel were going out of their way to be cooperative in the Whitewater investigation (Living History, p. 200). A January 10, 1996 Chicago Tribune *editorial stated, "[O]ne thing has become all too clear. Bill and Hillary Clinton, and their aides, have made a concerted effort to deceive official investigators and the American public with half truths and outright lies…"*

(Photo courtesy of MPTV.net, © 1965, Gabi Rona)

Hillary and Sgt. Schultz—separated at birth?

It appears I cooperated with this effort—to dispose of such files.

Hillary admitting, in a sworn statement, that she did shred some Whitewater documents, contradicting her earlier denials (Nightline, 01/30/96). *Hillary wrote in her autobiography, "We will never know whether releasing an inevitably incomplete set of personal documents to The Washington Post would have averted a special prosecutor"* (Living History, p. 216). *As Dick Morris explained, the reason the documents were "inevitably incomplete" was because she had shredded them* (Rewriting History, p. 162).

I, like everyone else, would like to know the answer about how those documents showed up, after all these years.

More on the magically reappearing billing records (Nightline, 01/30/96).

I tried to be as helpful as I could in their investigation efforts.

Mrs. Clinton claiming that she tried to be "helpful" in the search for the piece of evidence that proved she lied about her involvement in Whitewater (Online Newshour, PBS.org, 04/01/96).

[I] did not know how the [Rose Law Firm] billing records came to be found where they were found. I am pleased that they were found because they confirm what I have been saying.

Comments regarding the documents that were found in the White House residence, just outside her bedroom, about which she was later questioned by a grand jury (Frontline, 10/07/97).

How could this have happened?

Senator Clinton expressing her dismay about FBI documents, which had been missing for five years, suddenly turning up on the eve of Timothy McVeigh's execution (The Washington Times, 05/17/01). *Of course, no credible explanation has ever been given—at least by Hillary—as to how the missing White-*

water billing records, which had been missing for four years, turned up in the White House across from her bedroom in January 1996 (Shadow, p. 317).

Cattle Futures

I was lucky.

Hillary's explanation of how she turned a $1,000 investment in the cattle futures market into $100k, a profit of 10,000 percent, in just under one year (The First Partner, p. 108). *The late Barbara Olson pointed out that, had Hillary invested $1,000 in the first offering of Microsoft she would only have made $35,839 in eight years. "The premier technology investment of our times, therefore, pales in comparison to what she had made on the world's oldest commodity: livestock"* (Hell to Pay, p. 141).

"Tell me again, how much did I win?"

It really wasn't a risk, was it?

Hillary asking Jim McDougal a rhetorical question about her cattle futures profits, circa 1978, after she engaged him to prepare tax shelters because of her $100,000 profit (Arkansas Mischief, p. 167). The Journal of Economic Statistics *concluded that the odds of Hillary making the trades herself were one in 250 million.* (American Evita, p. 74). *During several of Hillary's most profitable trades, she was in Washington, D.C. serving as chairperson on the Legal Services Corporation* (American Evita, p. 74).

There's no evidence of that...No, I really don't believe that.

Hillary's lawyerly denial that she received special treatment in her cattle futures trades (The New York Times, 04/23/94). *After getting negative press once the cattle futures story came out, Clinton aide John Podesta said that there was no impropriety on Hillary's part. "The only appearance is being created by* The New York Times" (Hell to Pay, p. 138).

The large return on my investment was examined *ad infinitum* after Bill became president...The conclusion was that, like many investors at the time, I'd been fortunate.

Her explanation of her futures profits in her autobiography (Living History, p. 87). *On her 1980 tax return, Hillary reported a $1,000 loss. However, after her huge profit from these trades became public in 1994, the Clintons paid $14,615 in additional taxes, interest, and penalties. The brokers who assisted her in these trades were later prosecuted for conducting exactly the same kinds of trades as Hillary* (Rewriting History, p. 155).

Travelgate

We need those people out—we need our people in—we need the slots.

Hillary's memo to David Watkins regarding the Travel Office employees who were fired shortly thereafter (Hell to Pay, p. 242). *This prompted Mr. Watkins to write his famous memo: "We both knew that there would be hell to pay if...we failed to take swift and decisive action in conformity with the first lady's wishes [to resolve the Travel Office situation]"* (Hell to Pay, p. 244).

Get on it. Don't let this thing fester. Fix it. Deal with it.

Orders to the late Vince Foster, who, in turn, ordered David Watkins to proceed with the investigation and termination of the White House Travel Office employees (Hillary's Choice, p. 232).

[I] had no role in the decision to terminate the [Travel Office] employees.

Hillary's public story regarding the seven people fired from the White House Travel Office in 1993 (Hell to Pay, p. 245).

I was among the many people who were concerned about reports of financial mismanagement in the Travel Office, and I did express concerns, but the decisions about who should do what and when it should be done, those were all made by other people.

(CNN.com, 01/07/96). Hillary changes her story. Robert Ray, who took over as Independent Counsel after Ken Starr resigned, wrote, "The independent counsel concludes that Mrs. Clinton's sworn testimony that she had no input into Watkins' decision or role in the Travel Office firings is factually inaccurate." He went on to conclude, "Mrs. Clinton's input into the process was significant, if not the significant factor influencing the pace of events in the Travel Office firings and the ultimate decision to fire the employees" (ABCNews.com, 10/18/00).

If you read his memo, he doesn't say I directly told him anything.

More denials from Hillary regarding the Travel Office firings (The Wall Street Journal, 01/17/96). David Watkins also took notes from a telephone conversation with Hillary where "she conveyed to me in clear terms her desire for swift and clear action" (Shadow, p. 294).

I just don't have any memory of that.

Hillary's sworn statement regarding the Watkins memo which stated that it was she who wanted the White House Travel Office employees fired (The Limbaugh Letter quoting Newsweek, 02/96). Craig Livingstone, former bar bouncer and Hillary Clinton White House staffer, once told an FBI agent about testifying under oath: "Don't you know that truth is relative? Your testimony was your version of the truth. Truth is whatever you want it to be" (Unlimited Access, p. 134).

Before I came to the White House, I dealt with people in a very direct way. If something was on my mind, I said it.

Hillary explaining that she "expressed concern" regarding the way the White House Travel Office was run, but did not order the employees fired (Nightline, 01/30/96).

Monica Lewinsky

I have a pretty good antenna for people who are chauvinistic or sexist or patronizing toward women.

In an eerie coincidence, Hillary made this statement (speaking of former Representative Melvin Laird and how respectful he was towards young, female interns) just a few days before the Monica Lewinsky scandal hit Washington in January 1998 (Hillary's Choice, p. 64). Coed Hillary Rodham served as an intern to Representative Laird before going to law school.

[What] the president has told the nation is the whole truth and nothing but the truth.

To Matt Lauer in the early days of the Lewinsky scandal (The Today Show, 01/27/98). In 1994 Joe Klein, author of Primary Colors, wrote of the Clintons: "[A] clear pattern has emerged—of delay, of obfuscation, of lawyering the truth...With the Clintons, the story always is subject to further revision. The misstatements are always incremental. The misunderstandings are always innocent...Trust is squandered in dribs

Somehow this fellow made it past her antenna.

and drabs" (EtherZone.com, 06/28/00).

If all that were proven true, I think that would be a very serious offense. This is not going to be proven true.

Addressing Matt Lauer's hypothetical question of presidential infidelity (The Today Show, *01/27/98).*

Bill and I have been accused of everything, including murder, by some of the very same people who are behind these allegations. So from my perspective, this is part of a continuing political campaign against my husband.

More to Matt Lauer regarding the Lewinsky scandal, and the people who make up the "vast right-wing conspiracy" (The Today Show, *01/27/98).*

I think my husband has proven that he's a man who really cares about this country deeply and respects the presidency...and when it's all said and done, that's how most fair-minded Americans will judge my husband.

Early in the Clintons' first term, as they were being criticized on various subjects (Bill & Hillary, *p. 283). Hillary has never commented about the time that Bill was respecting the presidency by receiving oral sex from Monica Lewinsky while on the phone discussing U.S. troop movements in Bosnia.*

Bill told me that Monica Lewinsky was an intern he had befriended two years earlier...He said that she had misinterpreted his attention, which was something I had seen dozens of times before.

(Living History, *p. 441). After Kathleen Willey accused Clinton of groping her, several women who worked in the White House were upset, refusing to believe Clinton's denials. "One woman, a senior White House official, had heard from two colleagues who had experiences uncomfortably similar to what Willey described: innocent conversations that pivoted [into] instant fervid advances"* (The Survivor, *p. 229).*

He ministers to troubled people all the time...If you knew his mother you would understand it.

To Sidney Blumenthal regarding how Bill only "ministered" to Monica Lewinsky (A Vast Conspiracy, *p. 242*).

You stupid fucking moron. How could you risk your presidency for this?

Ever-supportive Hillary to her husband when the Monica Lewinsky scandal became public in January 1998 (NewsMax.com, 12/09/01).

[We] just stayed home and cleaned closets.

Explaining what she and Bill did the night of his deposition in the Paula Jones case (CBS Radio, 01/19/98). Hillary didn't mention if she also baked cookies and fixed tea that night, as well.

President Clinton "ministering" away in this infamous picture from 1996.

Well, I think people will remember that when Joe said that, the president said he agreed with him.

Explaining how happy she was that Al Gore selected Joe Lieberman to be his running mate in the 2000 election, even though it was Lieberman who harshly criticized President Clinton for his "immoral conduct" in the Lewinsky scandal (Newsmax.com, 08/09/00).

My husband may have his faults, but he has never lied to me.

To an advisor just hours before Bill supposedly confessed to her about his true relationship with Monica (Living History, p. 465).

I could hardly breathe. Gulping for air, I started crying and yelling at him. "What do you mean? What are you saying? Why did you lie to me?"

Hillary's "reaction" after Bill confessed his true relationship with the infamous intern (Living History, p. 466). Clinton reportedly told Monica Lewinsky that he had had "hundreds of affairs." He also told her that Kathleen Willey's sexual harassment allegation was ludicrous because, "he would never be interested in a small-breasted woman" (Uncovering Clinton, p. 148).

Hillary caught mid-gulp.

My husband is a good person. Yes he has weaknesses…But it is remarkable, given his background, that he turned out to be the kind of person he is…

(Sundaytimes.com, 08/08/99). A former Secret Service agent complained that after Clinton would greet female voters he would often "turn away and speculate under his breath about whether they gave good blow jobs or not" (The First Partner, p. 259).

You know, we did have a very good stretch—years and years of nothing...I thought this was resolved ten years ago.

Months after the impeachment trial, Hillary discusses her husband's past philandering and his relationship with Monica Lewinsky (Talk Magazine, 08/99). A Secret Service agent was quoted as saying they don't have a marriage, but a political alliance. "She portrayed herself as devastated by the revelations of Monica. I doubt she cared" (A Matter of Character, *p. 3*).

Ken Starr

Don't you dare show him the Lincoln Bedroom.

Hillary ordering a White House staffer to disregard President Clinton's offer to have Ken Starr tour the then-infamous room, during Whitewater negotiations between the Clintons and the Independent Counsel, circa 1996 (Washingtonpost.com, 06/13/99). During these negotiations, Starr had impressed the president with his enthusiasm and knowledge of the history of the White House. In an act of goodwill, Clinton ordered that Starr get a tour of the White House, and the Lincoln bedroom specifically.

The worst thing you can do now is roll over and play dead. Bill, you have got to come out and hammer Ken Starr.

Advice given to President Clinton the day of his mea culpa *to the nation confessing his improper relationship with Monica Lewinsky (Bill & Hillary, p. 27). Clinton's other advisors were telling him to be contrite and to apologize to the American people for lying to them for the previous eight months, but Hillary wanted him to come out swinging.*

I think a lot of this is prejudice against our state. They wouldn't do this if we were from some other state.

Just days before her husband was to testify before the grand jury regarding Lewinsky, Hillary thinks the investigation is due to evil white male Ken Starr's prejudice against Arkansans (The Washington Post, 08/12/98).

Well, it's your speech; you should say what you want to say.

Telling her husband to blast Ken Starr for the Lewinsky investigation, just before Clinton gave his four-minute mea culpa *speech to the American people on August 17, 1998* (The Breach, *p. 33*).

Why is Starr getting a free ride?...Everything we do gets put under a microscope, and look at this guy. No one says anything negative about him.

Fuming to aides after being compelled by Ken Starr to testify before the grand jury about the missing billing records (Shadow, *p. 317*). *At one meeting, President Clinton told staff members he wanted everyone in the Independent Counsel's office audited. When several people counseled him against this approach, Clinton slammed his fist down on the table and said: "I can do any goddamned thing I want. I'm president of the United States. I take care of my friends and I fuck with my enemies." (CapitolHillBlue.com, 04/08/99).*

If men like Starr...could ignore the Constitution and abuse power for ideological and malicious ends to topple a president, I feared for my country.

Hillary's great fear for her country (Living History, *p. 472*). *Keep in mind that she wrote this in 2003, well after the 9/11 attacks had killed nearly three thousand people in her "home" state of New York.*

Starr's distribution of his report was gratuitously graphic and degrading to the presidency...

Blaming Ken Starr, but not her husband, for degrading the presidency and the Constitution (Living History, *p. 475*).

Ken Starr uncovered evidence that caused Bill Clinton to be impeached and have his law license revoked, and *he* "ignored the Constitution?"

I remember when I read *The Autobiography of Benjamin Franklin*. I discovered things about Franklin's personal life that...I was shocked by.

Hillary explains that for great men, such as Ben Franklin and Bill Clinton, philandering is common (American Heritage, 12/94).

As I have long argued, the current ban on interstate shipment puts our local [New York wine] producers at a competitive disadvantage, and I am pleased that the U.S. Supreme Court held that such laws unconstitutionally discriminate against interstate commerce.

Statement of Senator Clinton regarding the Supreme Court victory of the wine producers to ship across state lines (Clinton.Senate.gov, 05/16/05). "As I have long argued?" "Our local wine producers?" Interestingly enough, Hillary's nemesis and evil white man Ken Starr was one of the attorneys who successfully represented the wine producers. It's probably just an oversight, but he has yet to receive a thank-you card from her office.

Impeachment

[Impeachment] is not just about my husband. It is about the Constitution.

To Democrats in Congress, urging them to "save the Constitution" by not voting with the evil Republicans for impeachment (Bill & Hillary, p. 310). In February 1999, on the same day the Senate voted to acquit her husband, Hillary held a strategy meeting in the White House to discuss her eventual run for senator of New York.

The case for impeachment was part of a political war waged by people determined to sabotage the president's agenda on the economy, education, Social Security, health care, the environment and the search for peace in Northern Ireland, the Balkans, and the Middle East...

(Living History, p. 489). Right. We would've had peace on Earth and an end to human suffering if only the GOP had ignored her husband's perjury and obstruction of justice.

Much of this is coming from right-wing elements that have been opposed to my husband...all his life. And I don't want them to win. And you shouldn't want them to win either. And I think it's important for the country that they not win.

Pleading to Congressman Jim Moran, D-VA, as he ponders whether to impeach President Clinton (The Breach, p. 105). *Many Congressional Democrats were seriously considering voting for impeachment but changed their minds after personal pleas such as this from Mrs. Clinton.*

Bill had been blindsided, and the unfairness of it all made me more determined to stand with him to combat the charges.

(Living History, *p. 442*). *She of course neglects to mention that her own political future was also at stake.*

A right-wing network was after his presidency...including perverting the Constitution.

Explaining to Barbara Walters about the un-fair-minded Republicans who impeached President Clinton (20/20, 06/08/03). *It's been revealed that Clinton used a cigar sexually on Monica, not to mention receiving oral sex from her after attending church on Easter Sunday* (The Starr Report, 09/11/98)—*and Hillary claims the* Republicans *are the perverts?*

[He's] the commander-in-chief, the president, the man I love.

Circa October 1998, Hillary urging Congressional Democrats to show loyalty by voting against impeachment (The Breach, p. 246). *Hamilton Jordan, former Chief of Staff in the Carter White House, wrote the following of Clinton-style loyalty: "The Clintons are not a couple but a business partnership, not based on love or even greed but on shared ambitions. Everywhere they go, they leave a trail of disappointed, disillusioned friends and staff members to clean up after them. The Clintons' only loyalty is to their own ambitions"* (The Wall Street Journal, 02/20/01).

Pardon Me?

Bill, you're out of your mind! You can't do this, you just can't do this.

Regarding the pardons and commuted sentences Bill Clinton awarded to convicted rapists and murderers during his final days as governor (Hillary's Choice, *p. 141*). *This was a precursor to the controversial pardons that Clinton granted in the final days of his presidency, in January 2001.*

I knew nothing about my brother's involvement in these pardons. I knew nothing about his taking money for his involvement...

Senator Clinton again utilizing the Sgt. Schultz defense, this time in connection to her brother selling presidential pardons (The Final Days, *p. 179*).

Hugh Rodham golfing with the president. In other news, four fried chickens were reported missing from the White House kitchen.

It's very hard to stop people who have no shame about what they're doing...[W]ho have never been acquainted with the truth.

A speech to Democratic supporters (The New York Times, *06/06/05*). *And if anyone is an authority on lack of shame, it's Hillary.*

I was very disturbed to learn that my brother...received fees in connection with two clemency applications, I believe that the payments should be returned immediately, and I understand he has taken steps to do so.

(USAToday.com, 02/22/01).

I did not know my brother was involved in any way in any of this.

Commenting on brother Hugh's involvement in the controversial pardon of alleged drug dealer Carlos Vignali, granted during Bill Clinton's final days in office (FoxNews.com, *08/08/01*). *Hugh Rodham received $200,000 for obtaining the pardon. When asked how he knew to contact the president for a pardon, Mr. Vignali said, "Word around prison was that it was the right time to approach the president"* (The Final Days, *p. 152*).

I have no opinion. I had no opinion before. I had no opinion at the time. I have no opinion now...[A]nd, you know, I really don't have any opinion about it.

The World's Smartest Woman expressing her opinion about the Marc Rich pardon (CNN.com, *01/29/01*).

[I] never knew about Marc Rich at all. You know, people would hand me envelopes, I would just pass them...I knew nothing about the Marc Rich pardon until after it happened.

Regarding her husband's pardon of Marc Rich, at the time #6 on the Justice Department's most-wanted list of international fugitives (NewsMax.com, *02/24/01*). *Carter White House Chief of Staff Hamilton Jordan writes, "It is incredible that the ethical atmosphere of the Clinton White House had sunk to a level whereby the constitutional power of a president to issue a pardon was*

discussed among Mr. Clinton and his White House staff as just one more perk of office" (The Wall Street Journal, 02/20/01).

I signed on to a bill that states an important principle that obviously is prospective and doesn't look back into previous administrations, and I thought that was a good idea.

Just two months after the controversial pardon of fugitive Marc Rich, Senator Clinton supports a bill regarding disclosures about future, and only future, presidential pardons (NewsMax.com, 03/31/01).

I did not play any role whatsoever. I had no opinion about it.

Regarding the New Square pardons that President Clinton granted to four Hasidic Jews on his last day in office (The Final Days, p. 145). These four residents of New Square, a community made up primarily of Russian Jewish immigrants, had been convicted of defrauding the government of $40 million.

Most people wouldn't view the government being bilked out of $40 million as a hoot. Here, Hillary laughs it up with young New Square members.

There was a meeting. I did sit in on it. That issue [of pardoning the convicts] was raised. It was referred to the president. I never made any view known one way or another at any time.

Hillary claiming to have said nothing about the New Square pardons during a meeting in the White House in December 2000. According to former Clinton aide George Stephanopoulos, "The fact that she didn't say a word [in this discussion] shows that she knew something was wrong with the meeting" (This Week, *02/25/01). Further questions of impropriety on Hillary's part were raised by the discovery that members of the New Square community voted for Hillary in the Senate election by 1400 to 12, a 99 percent margin of victory* (Townhall.com, *06/27/02).*

Looting & the Ws

Wouldn't it be hysterical if someone just happened to remove all the *W*s from the computer keyboards?

The outgoing First Lady ponders this thought out loud on their final evening in the White House (American Evita, *p. 5). Even though Democrats claimed there was no actual damage to the White House, a General Accounting Office investigation revealed that Clinton staffers caused $19,000 in various damages to the White House* (The Washington Post, *06/12/02).*

I can only say that all the gifts were appropriately dealt with, and we followed the same procedures that all presidents have followed.

Senator Clinton commenting on reports that they looted the White House and kept many undisclosed gifts (The Final Days, *p. 73, quoting the* New York Daily News). *According to Linda Tripp, when the Clintons entered the White House in 1993 the staff was ordered to not document many of the gifts they were receiving after the inauguration, in violation of federal laws* (Larry King Live, *02/09/01).*

I don't know why anybody is still talking about this...we followed every single law.

Another denial regarding the gifts controversy, where the Clintons took certain items from the White House to their multi-million dollar home in New York (The New York Post, 02/13/02). Once it was proved that they did take items home, Bill and Hillary were forced to return many of these gifts to the White House. Hillary chalked up this controversy to "a clerical error" (Living History, p. 439).

CHAPTER FIVE:
Those Evil Republicans

We didn't get any Eleanor. But we got a lot of Evita.

—Jim McDougal regarding Hillary comparing herself to Mrs. Roosevelt
(*The Washington Post*, 03/09/98)

Richard Nixon

I'm very regretful that others since then have not followed that kind of thoughtful, non-partisan, above the fray sort of approach.

Contrasting what she saw as the Republicans' biased and near-obsessive pursuit of her husband, with the "principled" approach she believed she and her colleagues on the staff of the Watergate House Judiciary Committee took in investigating President Nixon (Booknotes, 03/03/96).

He's pure evil.

A statement Hillary made about Nixon that demonstrated just how principled and "above the fray" she was (American Evita, p. 47). The late Barbara Olson wrote, "It is more than a little ironic that Hillary was a staffer on the House Judiciary Committee that prepared articles of impeachment against President Richard Nixon, because she's very much like the public's image of Nixon: ambitious, cold, ruthless, and willing to evade, stonewall, or even lie when it serves her purpose" (The Final Days, p. 13).

"He's pure evil?" In related news, the pot calls the kettle black.

[Impeachment should apply] to those offenses which proceed from the misconduct of public men...from the abuse or violation of some public trust.

Hillary, during Watergate, citing Alexander Hamilton in support of impeaching Richard Nixon (The Wall Street Journal, *09/11/98). Hillary also thought that President Nixon should be prosecuted for war crimes for his role in Vietnam. In other words, she argued forcefully for a broader definition of the legal justification for impeachment—a position that would come back to haunt her* (Hillary's Choice, *p. 90).*

I've always said I thought Richard Nixon absolutely made the right decision for the country by resigning and sparing the country a trial in the Senate and all the anguish that would have produced.

Hillary approving of Nixon's decision to resign from office in lieu of an impeachment trial, years before her husband put the country through the ordeal of one (A First Lady For Our Time, *p. 256).*

But when the shoe is on the other foot...

Your health-care reform legislation in 1973-74 was so good that we are using it as a blueprint for our own package. Had you survived in office, you would have been light years ahead of your time.

Hillary's words upon meeting President Nixon in 1994 at the Clinton White House (The New York Post, *04/07/04). This prompted a furious Nixon to later exclaim, "Maybe I could have [survived in office] if she hadn't been working to impeach me"* (Newsmax.com, *04/07/04).*

That fink! What did Tricky Dick have to say about me?

Early in Bill Clinton's first term, the co-president reacts to criticism from President Nixon (Clinton Confidential, *p. 365). In 1975 a Methodist minister named Vic Nixon married Bill and Hillary. She later quipped, "Never thought I'd be married by Nixon"* (American Evita, *p. 60).*

Ronald Reagan

[We] will always remember President Ronald Reagan for the way he personified the indomitable optimism of the American people, and for keeping America at the forefront of the fight for freedom for people everywhere.

Joint statement issued by President Bill Clinton and Senator Hillary Rodham Clinton on the occasion of President Reagan's death (CNN.com, *06/05/04).*

At least [President Reagan] had some core beliefs. They defied logic, but at least he had them.

During the 1992 campaign, the first lady of Arkansas criticizing President George Bush for his lack of core beliefs, as compared to Reagan (The Unique Voice of Hillary Rodham Clinton, *p. 62). After the 1992 Democratic Convention in New York City, President Reagan said, "They put on quite a production in New York a few weeks ago. You might even call it slick...Over and over they told us they are not the party they were. They kept telling us with straight faces that they're for family values, they're for a strong America, they're for less intrusive government. And they call me an actor" (ReaganLegacy.org, 01/12/06).*

Chelsea, we'll take a tour when someone decent lives there!

Circa 1985, Hillary's response when a young Chelsea asked if they could tour the White House during President Reagan's second term (Crossfire, p. 71). Corporate attorney Hillary also regularly reminded Chelsea that President Reagan and Vice President Bush were "rich people who just don't care about the problems of average Americans" (American Evita, p. 93).

This was the dark underbelly of the Republican Right, which rose to power with a very different public face: a sunny, self-confident Ronald Reagan.

Regarding the election of Reagan in 1980, (Living History, p. 423).

You ought to burn that goddamned thing...

Circa 1985, Hillary's comment to her Arkansas bodyguard when he proudly displayed a picture of himself with Nancy Reagan (Crossfire, p. 69).

Bush Forty-One

Fuck him, Bill. He's Reagan's goddamn vice president!

Hillary screaming her response to an invitation from Vice President George H. W. Bush to come to his home in Maine, circa 1984 (Crossfire, p. 69). According to former Clinton bodyguard L.D. Brown, "I don't believe Hillary hated [Bush] as much for whom he was as for what he was. Being the vice president of Ronald Reagan, the leader of the evil Republicans, was his greatest crime. Hillary actually hated Republicans" (Crossfire, p. 70).

When it's all stripped away, at the bottom, what we see is a failure of leadership, rooted in a very hollow sense of what politics is and can be.

Regarding Bush Forty-One's presidency (Hillary's Choice, p. 210).

He'll say anything to stay in office.

Accusing President Bush of lying about his knowledge in the Iran-Contra scandal, just days before the 1992 election (Hillary's Scheme, p. 45).

I don't understand why nothing's ever been said about a George Bush girlfriend. I understand he has a Jennifer, too.

During the 1992 campaign, spreading rumors about President Bush having a girlfriend named Jennifer, to counter publicity of Bill Clinton's affair with his Gennifer, Gennifer Flowers (NewsMax.com, 01/24/00).

I have no independent recollection of such a conversation.

Just days after spreading the rumors about President Bush, Hillary denies it happened, when asked about it (Hillary's Choice, p. 205).

I think those questions are out of bounds.

Senate candidate Hillary Clinton's response when asked about a rumored affair with Vince Foster (NewsMax.com, 01/24/00).

Bush Forty-Three

Words have a funny way of trapping our minds on the way to our tongues, but they are necessary means...for attempting to come to grasp with some of the inarticulate, maybe even inarticulable, things that we're feeling.

Hillary during her graduation speech, proving that public figures other than President G. W. Bush can be a bit "inarticulable" (Right Turns, p. 117).

God, what a jerk.

Hillary's reaction upon seeing George Bush's face on TV after his victory over Ann Richards in the 1994 Texas governor's race (American Evita, p. 143).

[The Bush] administration is run by people who have been obsessed with Saddam Hussein for more than a decade. And the fact that they could have been so poorly informed and prepared raises a lot of serious questions about the decisions they are making now.

Just three weeks before the capture of Saddam Hussein, Senator Clinton doing her best to raise the morale of the troops by telling the world that their leaders were uninformed and unprepared (Federalist.com, 11/25/03). When Senator Clinton flew to Iraq to visit the troops over a Thanksgiving weekend, some members of the military referred to her air transportation as "Broomstick One" (Reckless Disregard, p. 65).

Son of a bitch.

Hillary's reaction upon finding out President Bush upstaged her by making a surprise visit to the troops in Iraq over the 2003 Thanksgiving holiday (American Evita, p. 259).

The "jerk" and "son of a bitch" serving Thanksgiving dinner to the troops in Iraq.

This President Bush has not only been radical and extreme in terms of Democratic presidents but in terms of Republican presidents, including his own father. He's making America less free, fair, strong, and smart than it deserves to be in a dangerous world.

(HoustonChronicle.com, 12/05/03).

Now when I first got to the Senate...I quickly realized that [the Bush administration] intended to try to undo everything my husband had done. And I admit I take that kind of personally.

(C-SPAN, 04/09/05). No doubt the first thing President Bush did was give the Oval Office a good scrubbing.

Rudy Giuliani

Giuliani will screw you every time.

Senator Clinton upset at "America's Mayor" for upstaging her in a post-9/11 press conference (The Washington Post, 01/27/02).

Now we know why he likes opera.

Joking about Giuliani's troubled personal life (NYDailyNews.com, 05/14/03).

[Giuliani] has done a lot. But the Senate is a different job. You don't arrest a homeless person.

To David Letterman regarding Rudy Giuliani and his "Nazi-like" tactics of running New York City (The Late Show, 01/00). During this same appearance, to the surprise of many native New Yorkers, Hillary passed a fairly difficult NYC-related quiz that Letterman seemingly sprang on her. Later, however, Hillary's staff admitted that she was told the questions and answers in advance. This earned her the temporary nickname in the blogsphere of "Hillary Van Doren," in honor of Charles Van Doren, the most prominent person exposed in the famous 1950s quiz show scandals.

When you show up in the Senate, you can't hire, fire, and insult your colleagues if you don't get along with them...He gets angry quite often.

Complaining about Rudy's terrible temper, while on her "listening tour" of New York (Hillary's Scheme, p. 87). However, according to Christopher Andersen, author of American Evita, *Hillary had a bit of an anger problem herself: "The staff was not afraid of Bill Clinton, the staff was afraid of Hillary Clinton—they were terrified of her. She had a tremendous temper" (ET Online, 07/07/04).*

He's basically written off whole communities in the city that he's supposed to lead, what does that say about how people would be represented by him?

During the 2000 Senate campaign, she speaks of her then-opponent Rudy Giuliani, and his "failures" as a leader (NewsMax.com, 03/23/00).

The Louima and Diallo cases were not just horrific, but symptomatic of problems in the city's overall approach to policing.

More on Mayor Rudy Giuliani, the New York Police Department, and the "failure" of both institutions in serving New York City (Issues2000.org, 01/21/03). During this Senate race, she referred to an accidental police shooting as "the murder of Amadou Diallo" (The First Partner, p. 419).

The leadership in this city refuses to reach out, to work with a community that is in pain, to even acknowledge there is a problem.

Somewhat akin to her husband's famous "I feel your pain" line, Hillary attempts to make political hay by contrasting her recognition of the pain of New York's black community with opponent Rudy Giuliani's supposed lack of deftness in the area of race relations (NewsMax.com, 03/06/00). However, in terms of tangible results, Mayor Giuliani's reduction of crime in New York City by over 30 percent was of great benefit to the black community, as blacks in New York are disproportionately affected by crime.

The very picture of marital bliss: Hillary and Bill taking some time off.

Republicans Never Rest

I'd like some time off to sit on a beach or take a hike, but I don't think the Republicans ever rest.

(Newsmax.com, 07/25/04).

We believe passionately in this country and we cannot stand by for one more year and watch what is happening to it.

Regarding how the Clintons were about to rescue the country from George Bush and the evil Republicans (The Unique Voice of Hillary Rodham Clinton, *p. 36*).

When Bill won, it just absolutely amazed and infuriated some people because they thought they had a lock on the presidency forever.

Hillary explaining her theory on why the Republicans couldn't get over their obsessive hatred of her and her husband (Larry King Live, *06/10/03*).

I don't recognize this new brand of Republicanism that is afoot now, which I consider to be very reactionary, not conservative in many respects.

Another opinion of Republicans, circa the 1992 campaign (The Unique Voice of Hillary Rodham Clinton, *p. 61*). *In Hillary's mind, the radical right had taken over the party by 1992, even though Bush Forty-One was far less conservative than Ronald Reagan.*

Before this is over, they'll attack me, they'll attack you, they'll attack your cat, they'll attack your goldfish.

To Chelsea, early in the 1992 campaign, regarding the "lies" the evil Republicans will be spreading about the entire Clinton family (Bill & Hillary, *p. 18*).

What are you doing inviting these people into my home? These people are our enemies! They are trying to destroy us!

To a White House aide when she heard that—gasp!—Republicans had been invited to an upcoming event, circa 1993 (The Survivor, *p. 99*).

In 1980, the Republicans started the negative advertising...What Bill doesn't understand is, you've gotta do the same thing: pound the Republican attack machine and run against the press.

(Hillary's Choice, p. 12). Since it was Ronald Reagan who ran for the presidency on the Republican ticket in 1980, this could be one of the reasons why Hillary despised Reagan. In Hillary's view it was Reagan who invented negative campaign advertising for having the audacity to criticize Jimmy "Killer Rabbit" Carter's less-than-stellar presidential record. (Readers unfamiliar with the use of "killer rabbit" in connection to President Carter should search for it on the Internet. A fun tale awaits).

[The Republicans] will have hundreds and thousands of people in the galleries just for the purpose of disrupting our convention.

To Dick Morris prior to the 1996 Democratic Convention (Shadow, p. 335). Hillary felt that some "hippie-looking" people who had heckled Bill at a Democratic fundraiser were really Republican spies. She was very concerned the same thing would happen at the upcoming convention (Shadow, p. 335).

I think it will be very difficult, because [The Republicans] are a very disciplined, polished machine which intimidates opposition. Still, there comes a time when the truth has to count for something.

Senator Clinton opines about honesty and the Democrat's chances for victory in the 2004 Presidential election against Karl Rove and the evil Republicans (Newsmax.com, 09/15/03). When a younger Hillary learned the Republicans had been effectively using negative campaign ads she said, "We need to learn how the bad boys do it" (Hillary's Choice, p. 146).

But you know, you have got to hand it to them. These [Republicans] are ruthless and they are relentless.

Hillary addresses a crowd of Democrats at a private L.A. fundraiser, and condemns her favorite enemy, "the evil Republicans" (MSNBC.com, 10/28/02). In the 1990s, prior to becoming a multi-millionaire with homes in Georgetown and Chappaqua but not before working as a corporate lawyer on the board of three major corporations, Hillary had said, "The 1980s were about acquiring—acquiring wealth, power, privilege" (The Washington Post, 05/06/93).

I love watching Republicans squirm. They are great at dishing it out, but they can't take it when the truth is pointed out to them.

(The Unique Voice of Hillary Rodham Clinton, p. 62). According to Bernie Nussbaum, he and Hillary shared the view that "you should do harm to your enemies" (Shadow, p. 247). This is the same Mr. Nussbaum who was forced to resign over allegations of improper conduct in the Whitewater investigation.

[Republicans] want to weaken government to the point it can do little more than fund the military, build some highways, and do a few other things...like drilling in the Arctic National Wildlife Refuge.

At the Minnesota DFL Hubert Humphrey Dinner (C-SPAN, 04/09/05). With record numbers of the Americans employed by the government and the price of oil skyrocketing, perhaps Hillary should consider some of these ideas.

[Republicans] seemed to believe that old-fashioned rugged individualism was all that mattered...except when, of course, their supporters wanted special legislative favors.

Senator Clinton charging that Republican lawmakers were allowing financial supporters to influence their policy decisions (Living History, p. 291). Marc Rich, Carlos Vignali, and Hugh Rodham could not be reached for comment.

The Vast Right-Wing Conspiracy...

The great story for anybody willing to find it, and write about it, and explain it, is this vast right-wing conspiracy that has been conspiring against my husband since the day he announced for president.

In the midst of the Lewinsky scandal, Hillary makes "the mother of all stupid quotes" (The Today Show, 01/27/98). Former Clinton official Mickey Kantor said of the Clinton-Lewinsky scandal, "It's his own fault. No one did this to him. He did it to himself." (Legacy, p. 170).

That'll teach them to fuck with us.

To aides, immediately following her "vast right-wing conspiracy" charge on national television (The Case Against Hillary Clinton, p. 162).

It has been clear to me for a number of years that there really is a vast, right-wing conspiracy. My only regret was using the word "conspiracy" because there is absolutely nothing secret about it.

A speech before a group of law students (CNSNews.com, 08/02/03).

Do you remember I once mentioned the vast right-wing conspiracy? Some doubted me.

Complaining of Republican partisanship while speaking to the leftist group Take America Back (The Washington Post, 06/07/04). *Hillary sees groups such as Take America Back as centrist organizations. Their 2005 conference included such middle-of-the-road luminaries as Howie "The Scream" Dean and Ariana Huffington, who during a two-year period reportedly paid only $771 in personal income taxes, despite owning a $7 million home.*

...And Their Evil Minions in the Press

It's hurting so bad, Carolyn. The press doesn't believe you have any feelings. They sure don't believe in the Bible.

To a friend during the 1992 campaign regarding the media's (which Hillary believed was controlled by the Republican establishment) reaction to the Clintons's denials concerning Bill's womanizing while governor of Arkansas (Bill & Hillary, p. 239).

They are so snotty about people who don't live in Georgetown...

Hillary regarding the Washington establishment and The Washington Post *in particular* (The Choice, p. 102). *In her high school yearbook, Hillary wrote as her life's goal, "Marry a senator and settle down in Georgetown." She now lives in...Georgetown* (Hell to Pay, p. 25).

This personal, vicious hatred that for the time being is being aimed at the president, and, to a lesser extent, myself, is very dangerous for our political process.

Circa 1994, Hillary felt that any criticism of her, or her health care plan, was dangerous to democracy (The Washington Post, 08/19/94). *In 1996, while* on a European trip, Hillary was asked a question regarding one of the many scandals surrounding the Clinton administration. The reporter who asked this question was later confronted by Hillary's press secretary who shouted, "The first lady was furious that you asked this question…she expected more of you" (Hillary's Choice, p. 290).

I can't take this anymore. How can I go on? How can I?

Circa January 1996, her reaction when columnist William Safire wrote that she was a "congenital liar" for all her false statements and explanations regarding Whitewater and the White House Travel Office firings (Washingtonpost.com, 06/14/99).

I cannot take Mr. Safire seriously. I worked with the committee that impeached Nixon. Safire worked for Nixon. As best as I can tell, he is still working for the Nixon administration.

Hillary using guilt by association to explain why Safire's opinions should not be taken seriously (The New York Times, 01/96). Luckily for Hillary, her personal associations are so above reproach that no one could seriously question her opinions on the same basis.

There hasn't been anybody whose life has been picked apart and distorted as much as mine. I don't think New York can be any worse.

Regarding all the negative press she was subjected to while campaigning in New York (BBC News Online, 10/25/00).

He assails me for something nearly every day, and I feel sorry for him.

Hillary expressing her opinion of Fox newsman Bill O'Reilly, because he had the temerity to question her ethics and criticize her statements and behavior (Capitol Gang, 12/15/01).

It doesn't ever seem to end. If a couple days go by and they haven't heard anything they can talk about, they make something up. It never ends.

First-victim Hillary Rodham Clinton charging that the press invented stories to discredit or hurt her (The Washington Post, 01/27/02).

I mean you've got a conservative and right-wing press presence with really nothing on the other end of the political spectrum.

Complaining about the "right-wing" media (C-SPAN, 01/19/97).

I respect you, Dan.

Speaking to soon-to-be-disgraced CBS News anchor Dan Rather (60 Minutes II, 05/26/99). *This "objective" reporter once told Bill Clinton, "If we could be one-hundredth as great as you and Hillary have been in the White House, we'd take it right now and walk away winners" (MediaResearch.org, 12/10/98).*

Tom, Dan, and Peter, three prime examples of Hillary's "right-wing press."

CHAPTER SIX:
Saint Hillary

If people disagree with one another, let's do it in a civil,
polite way. Let's not call each other names.

–Hillary Clinton (*The Unique Voice of Hillary Rodham Clinton*, p. 189)

Seventy Times Seven

I have to confess that it's crossed my mind that it's crossed my mind that you could not be a Republican and a Christian.

During a speech to religious leaders, Hillary states that from time to time she's felt this way towards Republicans (CNN.com, 02/17/97). However, she also admitted the Clintons have "spent a lot of time in the last several years demonizing people with whom we do not agree politically."

A beatifically draped Hillary gives an audience to her disciples.

I've got to take this. I have to take this punishment. I don't know why God has chosen this for me, but He has...God is doing this, and He knows the reason.

To a friend a few days after Bill confessed his relationship with Monica, August 1998 (WashingtonPost.com, 06/14/99). Many Democrats in the House and Senate were privately hoping he would resign, sparing them from having to call for his resignation. However, in the 1998 midterms, the Democrats unexpectedly picked up some seats. A joyful Hillary assumed there would be no impeachment inquiry. "It looks like nothing is going to happen to us. Isn't that great?" (The Wall Street Journal, 12/08/98).

In the Bible it says they asked Jesus how many times you should forgive, and he said seventy times seven. Well, I want you all to know that I'm keeping a chart.

(BrainyQuotes.com, 01/21/06).

The only way to make a difference is to acquire power.

Hillary Rodham to a friend shortly before starting law school (Bill & Hillary, p. 100). A reverend friend of Hillary's said, "My sense of Hillary is that she realizes...that you cannot depend on the basic nature of man to be good...You have to use power" (New York Times Magazine, 05/23/93).

[I] hope that tonight you will recognize that this battle over choice is a much wider struggle than just what happened in *Roe v. Wade*. It's also part of an effort to turn back on evidence and science. You know I have come to believe that the other side wants to turn Washington into an evidence-free zone.

A speech to pro-abortion group NARAL (FriendsofHillary.com, 01/22/04).

There is an opportunity for people of good faith to find common ground in this debate—we should be able to agree that we want every child born in this country to be wanted, cherished and loved.

Supposedly moving to the center regarding the abortion debate (NYTimes.com, 01/25/05). In April of 2005, Newsmax reported that Senator Clinton refused to meet with members of a pro-life group. The organization's spokesman said, "It now seems that the statements Senator Clinton made, concerning finding common ground on abortion, were politically motivated and not sincere" (Newsmax.com, 04/26/05).

The Holy Father was a beacon of light not just for Catholics, but for all people.

Joint statement of Bill & Hillary after the death of Pope John Paul II (Newsmax.com, 04/03/05).

Bill and Hillary pictured with one of those wacky "Christian conservatives" who oppose abortion.

Bill's Women—Her Cross to Bear

Anybody who knows my husband knows that he bends over backwards to help people who are in trouble and is always willing to listen to their problems.

Hillary claiming that Bill was only trying to "help" Gennifer Flowers by calling her during the 1992 campaign (The Unique Voice of Hillary Rodham Clinton, p. 52).

These women are all trash. Nobody's going to believe them.

Her opinion of the many women who claimed they had a "personal relationship" with Governor Clinton (Bill & Hillary, p. 220). During this campaign, Hillary sent out a group of investigators known as the "truth squad" to discourage many of Bill's former lovers from going public.

The daughter of Willie Horton?

This is the daughter of Willie Horton.

Brushing off rumors of her husband having an improper relationship with Arkansas nightclub siger Gennifer Flowers (Vanity Fair, 06/92). *By invoking Willie Horton, Hillary was attempting to imply that the Republicans were injecting another scandalous lie into a presidential campaign, just as Hillary believed they had done in the 1988 presidential race* with Michael Dukakis.

What the fuck do you think you're doing? I know who that whore is. I know what she's here for. Get her out of here.

To President-Elect Clinton as she spots him talking to one of his reputed girlfriends at a going-away celebration the day they left Little Rock for Washington, D.C. in January 1993 (Inside the White House, p. 243). *Oops, that must have been number seventy times seven plus one.*

Goddamn it Bill, how long do you expect me to put up with this shit?

One of their many fights concerning Governor Clinton's womanizing (Bill & Hillary, p. 202). *Former Arkansas state auditor Julia Hughes Jones said that Hillary was not only aware of Bill's womanizing, she enabled it. "Every time he was out and Hillary knew where he went, she would call behind him to see what she needed to do to take care of it"* (The American Spectator, 08/96).

The sorry damn son of a bitch!

Hillary's reaction upon being informed that Bill was missing from the governor's mansion in the middle of the night because "he had gone for a drive" (Inside the White House, p. 240). *The troopers eventually tracked him down at the apartment of one of his paramours* (Inside the White House, p. 241).

You are a real shit, do you know that, Bill? Christ, a real shit.

A fight over his affairs (Bill & Hillary, *p. 132*). *After* The American Spectator *and* The Los Angeles Times *detailed how Bill used state troopers to procure women for him, Clinton aide Betsey Wright said of the troopers, "As far as I can tell, they're telling the truth"* (American Evita, *p. 136*).

Come on, Bill, put your dick up. You can't fuck her here.

To Governor Clinton, after catching him talking to an attractive woman at a political rally (Inside the White House, *p. 243*). *In one of her books Hillary wrote, "Bill and I worked hard at our marriage with a great deal of mutual respect and deepening love for each other"* (It Takes a Village, *p. 43*).

"If you know what's good for you, bub, you'll stop staring at that woman's...eyes."

There is no way I'm going to let you read that. That's as good as admitting you're guilty.

Telling President Clinton not to read the following statement, which would have settled the Paula Jones lawsuit: "She did not engage in any improper or sexual conduct. I believe her to be a truthful and moral person" (Bill & Hillary, p. 289). Because Hillary would not let Bill accept this deal, years later the world became aware of the name Monica Lewinsky.

Bill has talked so much about Juanita.

On the way to a political gathering, Hillary to her limo driver, anxious to meet a woman named Juanita Hickey, now Juanita Broaddrick ("An Open Letter to Hillary Clinton: Do You Remember?" by Juanita Broaddrick, 10/15/00). Ms. Broaddrick claims that—several weeks before this encounter with Hillary— Bill Clinton raped her in a Little Rock hotel room.

Bill, now be sure and point Juanita out.

Hillary instructing her husband, while en route to the same rally, so she can have a word with Ms. Broaddrick (Bill & Hillary, p. 165).

I am so happy to meet you. I want you to know that we appreciate everything you do for Bill. Everything you do for Bill.

To Juanita, just weeks after Bill Clinton allegedly raped her (Hell to Pay, p. 308). Ms. Broaddrick later said of this meeting, "I understood perfectly what she was saying. I knew exactly what she meant—that I was to keep my mouth shut." Juanita also said that Hillary "was not going to let [the rape] get in the way. At that moment I knew what Hillary was capable of doing. And I could see in her eyes that she wasn't doing it for her husband. She wasn't even doing it for them. She was doing it for Hillary Rodham" (American Evita, p. 68).

I can see [him] any time I want to. I can look out the window and see Bill.

Hillary proudly telling a woman's magazine in 1993 how close her office was to the Oval Office (Ladies Home Journal, 08/93). By 1995 her office was moved to another part of the White House, the better not to see a certain intern delivering pizza to the Oval Office.

[He's a] hard dog to keep on the porch.

Regarding her husband's womanizing (BBC News Online, 10/25/00).

I am proud that my husband has stood up as president to confront the violence and to protect American women.

Regarding Bill Clinton's position on the issue of violence against women (Issues2000.org 01/21/03). When Bill Clinton saw that Juanita Broaddrick had a swollen lip after he raped her, he advised, "You'd better put some ice on that"(The Wall Street Journal, 02/19/99).

(Photo courtesy of Sherri Martin, © 2005.)

After touring the Clinton Library with author Candice Jackson (middle), Kathleen Willey (left) and Juanita Broaddrick (right) were shocked—shocked—to discover virtually no information about how Bill Clinton negatively impacted their lives.

Childcare, Clinton style.

It's for the Children

I want to be a voice for America's children.

Explaining her desire to care for "the children" (Hillary's Choice, *p. 86).*

I knew right away that I had to go to work for her.

Speaking of Marian Wright Edelman, the founder of the Children's Defense Fund (Hell To Pay, *p. 100). An avowed socialist, Edelman was Hillary's mentor. She felt that the "crusade of the children" could be used to bring about social change in the United States. "When you talked about poor people or black people, you faced a shrinking audience...I got the idea that [using] children might be a very effective way to broaden the base for change"—Marian Edelman (Quoted in* Hell To Pay, *p. 100).*

You sold out, you motherfucker, you sold out!

Circa 1970, congressional staffer Hillary Rodham yelling at prominent Democrat lawyer Joseph Califano, who was representing Coca-Cola executives

testifying on Capitol Hill regarding child labor issues (Inside: A Public and Private Life, p. 213). *Hillary's absolute self-righteousness strangely parallels Jimmy Carter's view of those who disagreed with him. "In later years it would be said that Carter judged people harshly according to whether they agreed with him, taking disagreements as a personal moral affront rather than allowing for honest difference of opinion"* (The Real Jimmy Carter, pp. 16-17).

I have to be strident or partisan or harsh to attract coverage...But to just go around making positive proposals on women and children doesn't bring any media coverage.

Whining to Dick Morris about a lack of national media exposure (Rewriting History, p. 125). *Morris goes on to write, "If* The New York Times *and* The Washington Post *weren't going to cover her speeches, the* Jackson Clarion Ledger *or the* Memphis Commercial Appeal *would. But Hillary didn't give a damn about that kind of coverage. She wanted the big spotlight, big coverage on the national stage"* (Rewriting History, pp. 125-126).

I just became more and more convinced that this is a campaign that needs to be made...I believe if we work together, we really can make a difference for the children and families in New York.

Hillary announcing her Senate candidacy (The Hillary Trap, pp. 163-164).

I want to get this shit over with and get these damn people out of here.

Hillary overheard on the governor's mansion intercom as some preschoolers posed on the mansion lawn for a photograph (The First Partner, p. 192).

It made a difference to Elian Gonzalez!

When it comes to White House interns though, that's a different story.

I don't believe [children] are ready for sex or its potential consequences...and I think we need to do everything in our power to discourage sexual activity and encourage abstinence.

(It Takes a Village, *p. 161).*

I think it does take a village to raise a child, and I think it takes Democrats to raise our hopes again.

(C-SPAN, 04/09/05).

You know, it's amazing to me that people actually stop at stop signs, that they do feed their children.

Talking about the importance of discipline (The Choice, *p. 136). With this low view of the average person, is there anything that Hillary trusts people to do for themselves in her "village?"*

Well, I am a fan of a lot of the social policies that you find in Europe...

Stating her affinity for Europe's cradle-to-grave welfare policies (Booknotes, *03/03/96).*

When I went to France... I saw what happens when a country makes caring for children a top priority.

Hillary again stating her opinion that Americans should emulate Europe's social welfare policies, particularly France's child-care system (The Hillary Trap, *p. 168). Of that system, Katrin Bennhold of the* International Herald Tribune *has written: "Illiteracy and poor French language skills are still common among immigrants, especially mothers who tend to be trapped inside the home, intensifying their alienation...The fathers, the traditional family authorities, often work long hours and do not see much of the children—and*

then find themselves stripped of their way of disciplining their children who challenge them by citing recent French legislation against beating in the home" (International Herald Tribune, 11/14/05).

I must say, we're hoping to have another child.

Hillary confides to a journalist before the 1996 election that she and Bill were talking about adopting a baby (Hell to Pay, p. 1). Because Hillary had the image of being a cold, arrogant, power-hungry attorney—imagine that!—the Clinton White House leaked this story to try to soften her negative public persona. After Bill Clinton's re-election was assured, the story of the "baby adoption" magically went away (Hell to Pay, pp. 1-2).

If the wrong side wins in this war on children, what will be lost is our notion of who we are as a people and what we stand for as a society.

Attacking the Republicans over their welfare reform plan—the one which her husband Bill Clinton eventually signed (Slander, p. 21). At the time, Hillary felt that any kind of welfare reform plan was an attack on children.

"By the way, I better not ever hear of *you* having another child!"

I supported welfare reform in the Clinton administration and I took enormous heat for that.

Hillary practicing a bit of revisionist history regarding her position on welfare reform, once the plan became a success (The Washington Times, *08/18/02*).

Our liberal friends are just going to have to understand that we have to go for welfare reform—for eliminating the welfare entitlement...I'm not going to listen to them or be sympathetic to them.

Engaging in even more revisionism, while positioning herself as taking a courageous stand against members of her own party (Hillary's Choice, *p. 289*).

We're not interested in social reconstruction; it's human reconstruction.

Hillary's famous 1969 Wellsley graduation speech (TheNewAmerican.com 07/12/93). In 1988, while head of the New World Foundation, Hillary gave a grant, via a conduit, of $5,000 to the Marxist FMLN of El Salvador to aid their efforts at "human reconstruction." According to Joe Cortina, an intelligence analyst specializing in El Salvador, "People need to understand the full impact of what Mrs. Clinton has done in supporting the FMLN. This is a full-fledged terrorist group that has killed and mutilated little children...You can maim a lot of kids for $5,000" (TheNewAmerican.com, 07/12/93).

She's All About Values

The media misunderstand me. I am actually very traditional in most of my beliefs, especially social issues.

To Clinton aide David Gergen when he asked if she was pulling Bill Clinton too far to the left (Eyewitness To Power, *pp. 267-268*).

Marriage has got historic, religious and moral content that goes back to the beginning of time, and I think a marriage is...between a man and a woman.

Hillary's opinion of gay marriage (AndrewSullivan.com, 04/27/00).

One of the most important initiatives I worked on as first lady and am proud to continue to champion in the Senate is the prevention of teen pregnancy. I worked alongside my husband who launched the National Campaign to Prevent Teen Pregnancy in the mid-1990s.

From a speech to the Family Planning Providers of New York (Clinton.Senate.gov, 01/24/05). Her husband certainly helped contribute to preventing teen pregnancy by promoting the idea that oral sex is not really "sex," a position he famously adopted to argue against perjury charges in the Lewinsky investigation. A recent study by the Centers for Disease Control and Prevention finds that teenagers of today have a much more casual opinion of oral sex than previous generations, and that more than one-half of 15- to 19-year-olds are engaging in the activity (USA Today, 10/19/05).

I for one respect those who believe with all their heart and conscience that there are no circumstances under which abortion should be available.

In a speech to the annual conference of the Family Planning Advocates of New York State (NYTimes.com, 01/24/05).

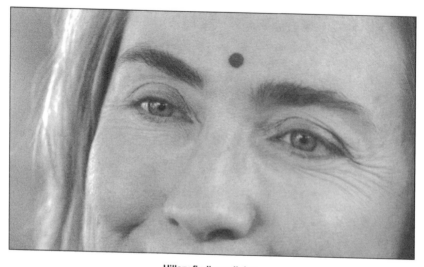

Hillary finding religion.

There are a number of forces at work in our society that would try to turn back the clock and undermine a woman's right to choose, and [we] must remain vigilant.

Candidate Clinton, during a televised debate with her Republican opponent Rick Lazio (Issues2000.org, 10/08/00).

It is a violation of human rights when women are denied the right to plan their own families...

From a speech in Beijing (Speech to United Nations 4th World Conference on Women, 09/05/95). Just to recap so it is perfectly clear to everyone how consistent Hillary is on this issue, she "respects" the members of the pro-life movement "who believe with all their heart" that abortion should not be legal, even though these same people are a "force at work in our society" that is trying to "turn back the clock" by advocating a "violation of human rights." Got it?

I have said many times that I can support a ban on late-term abortions, including partial-birth abortions, so long as the health and life of the mother is protected.

From her debate with Ric Lazio (Issues 2000, 10/08/00). Three years later Hillary would change course and vote against the Partial Birth Abortion Ban Act, a bill to outlaw the termination of late-term pregnancies. The bill was co-sponsored by forty-five senators and eventually passed in by a lopsided, bipartisan vote of 64-33 (Senate.gov, 03/13/03).

Character is one of the anchors of society. And when we talk about character we don't just mean talk, we mean action.

(The Unique Voice of Hillary Rodham Clinton, p. 188).

The office of the president is such that it calls for a higher level of conduct than expected from the average citizen of the United States.

Watergate staff attorney Hillary Rodham wrote that a president can be im-

peached, even though he does not engage in criminal offenses (Kansas City Star, *10/11/98*).

[W]hat we have in effect done is get used to more and more deviant behavior around us, because we haven't wanted to deal with it. But—by gosh!—it is deviant! It is deviant if you have any standards by which you expect to be judged.

Criticizing the lowering standards of societal behavior (New York Times Magazine, *05/23/93*). "At one point the president inserted a cigar into Monica Lewinsky's vagina, then put the cigar in his mouth and said: 'It tastes good'" (The Starr Report, *09/11/98*).

Russ, live in the real world!

Hillary screams at Senator Russ Feingold, after hearing about the restrictions to fundraising due to the McCain-Feingold campaign finance law (Newsmax.com, 07/19/02).

It's important to have core principles and values, but if you're going to be active in policy and politics, you have to be a realist.

Hillary talks about the importance of being flexible in your core beliefs (The Limbaugh Letter, *09/02*).

Research shows the presence of women raises the standards of ethical behavior and lowers corruption.

Hillary Clinton pontificating to a forum at New York University that

Mr. President, please don't tell us where that cigar has been.

female "leaders," such as herself, are less prone to corruption than their male counterparts (The Washington Square News, 03/08/05). *Regarding this assertion by Hillary, Dick Morris quipped, "Maybe women are more honest, but Hillary sure drags down the average" (Condi v. Hillary, p. 164).*

I think that the stakes have been raised on the partisanship. There are so many people who shoot before they aim. They don't get the facts. They're quick to, you know, make outrageous statements and judgments about other people. I don't think it's good for the country...

Regarding the so-called "poisonous" atmosphere in Washington (Booknotes, 03/03/96). She made this comment almost two years before the Monica Lewinsky scandal. Years later, Senator Clinton would imply "Bush knew" about the attacks of 9/11 but did nothing to stop them (CNN.com, 05/18/02).

Making the World a Better Place

Ever since I was a little girl, I've tried to do what's right.

(Larry King Live, 06/10/03). *Juanita Broaddrick might disagree.*

"Excuse me, sister, we got separated from my husband while touring your nunnery—I suggest we find him fast!"

You have to restrain yourself, Mr. President.

Senator Clinton's advice to President Bush regarding his judicial nominees (Human Events, 05/30/05). *Too bad she never thought to give the same advice to her husband.*

We know that if it could happen there—in broad daylight—it could happen anywhere. This is a crime against all women—everywhere. And so we have to say enough is enough. This violence is unacceptable and it must stop.

Senator Clinton regarding the sexual assaults caught on videotape at the Puerto Rican Day Parade in New York City in 2001 (United Press International, 06/23/01). *On the other hand, she could have been referring to the Clinton White House. In his best-selling book, Robert "Buzz" Patterson wrote that President Clinton once groped a female steward on Air Force One. She was very upset and demanded an apology from the president. After being confronted, Clinton personally apologized to her. Had a military officer done the same thing, he would have been jailed* (Dereliction of Duty, pp. 86-87).

We've had a steep increase in the number of reported rapes here in New York...

Senator Clinton announcing a new federal program for increased funding for DNA rape kits in New York (NewsMax.com, 04/29/02). *Coincidentally, Bill Clinton opened his office in Harlem nine months earlier in August of 2001.*

We will never build enough prisons to end our crime problem.

(Political rally in San Francisco, 09/13/96). So let's get this straight, the World's Smartest Woman wants the government to pay for test kits for rape victims, but she doesn't believe it should build the prisons needed to keep violent criminals locked up in the first place. Well, at least she's consistent—Hillary is "pro-victim" in every sense of the word.

All women who care about equality of opportunity, about integrity, and morality in the workplace, are in Professor Hill's debt.

From her speech at the 1992 ABA luncheon (The Real Anita Hill, p. 12). Who but trial lawyers would pay attention to Hillary Clinton opining on the importance of integrity and morality?

[She has] transformed consciousness and changed history with her courageous testimony.

Praising Ms. Hill, since she had the courage to accuse Clarence Thomas of sexual harassment (Legacy, p. 149). Also at the same luncheon, Hillary went on to say, "As women and as lawyers, we must never again shy away from raising our voices against sexual harassment." That explains the yelling that came out of the White House residential quarters during the 1990s.

I have a deep, abiding sense of obligation...I can't help wanting to do something about it.

Hillary gives her opinion about "public service" (The Unique Voice of Hillary Rodham Clinton, p. 69).

Hillary, as the obligation overwhelms her.

[Bill] and I really are bound together in part because we believe we have an obligation to give something back and to be part of making life better for other people.

After taking office from the evil Republicans in the 1992 election, Saint Hillary and her husband aim to save the country (The Choice, p. 134).

I have a burning desire to do what I can, a desire to make the world around me...better for everybody.

When asked about her ambitions and goals (The Unique Voice of Hillary Rodham

Clinton, p. 70). *However, when Hillary found out that White House staff member Chris Emery had helped former First Lady Barbara Bush with her computer, she promptly had him fired* (Hell To Pay, p. 240).

Not Just Sainted, but Crowned

The idea of hard-core Republican partisans rummaging through our lives...and harassing our friends on the flimsiest of excuses infuriated me.

(Living History, p. 297).

They can't really take me on, on the issues...so they practice what I call the politics of personal destruction.

While on her book tour in Europe, Hillary complains about those awful Republicans (Newsmax.com, 07/07/03).

We have to destroy her.

Regarding Gennifer Flowers' allegations of her affair with Bill (The Final Days, p. 13). *Anthony Pellicano, the private investigator used by the Clintons to investigate Ms. Flowers, was arrested in 2003 for threatening a reporter and is currently in prison for weapons violations. He once told* The Los Angeles Times, *"I only use intimidation and fear when I absolutely have to"* (Newsmax.com, 11/12/03).

Why should my daughter not have a pool just because my husband is governor?

Asking Dick Morris in 1985 why various "Friends of Bill" can't finance a swimming pool at the governor's mansion (The Final Days, p. 62). *This was shortly after Hillary made $100,000 in the cattle futures market. Paying for the pool themselves must not have occurred to Arkansas's first family.*

Have you ever seen anyone lose their temper? And how people lose control of their good sense in moments of passion?

After Bill lost the 1980 election for governor, Hillary explained that the voters of Arkansas had a temper tantrum, and were not thinking logically (First In His Class, p. 393).

I'm not interested in attending a lot of funerals around the world.

Hillary shutting down rumors about her desire to be vice president in the Clinton administration (Clinton Confidential, *p. 312*).

You know, I'm going to start thanking the woman who cleans the rest room in the building that I work in. You know, maybe that sounds kind of stupid, but on the other hand I want to start seeing her as a human being.

A speech given just a few weeks before she directed the White House Travel Office employees to be fired (New York Times Magazine, 05/23/93). *Apparently, it didn't occur to Hillary before this epiphany that most people already see maids, janitors, and other blue-collar workers as human beings.*

Time Magazine thinks I would be a good chief of staff.

Floating the idea to Dick Morris early in the Clinton administration, despite the anti-nepotism law forbidding family members from holding key administration jobs (Hillary's Choice, *p. 225*).

Do you know why these reporters keep attacking us? Keep investigating us? Because they're jealous. We are the same age as they are. We're all boomers. They don't have to get jealous of Bush or Reagan. They're too old. But we are the same age as they are and they can't get over the fact that we're here [in the White House] and they're not.

In the first term Hillary opines why the Clintons were getting criticized by the press (Rewriting History, *p. 60*). *According to a Democratic official, "She really does have a feeling that if you are not with us, then you are against us"* (Absolute Power, *p. 86*).

I will dress as I please.

Circa 1995, Hillary dismisses Dick Morris's advice to dress in friendlier, less lawyerly clothes (Guardian.co.uk, The Guardian, 07/12/99).

That's the way I want to be addressed from here on.

After the 1992 election, she makes it clear to her staff that she wants to be known only as Hillary Rodham Clinton and no longer as Mrs. Bill Clinton or Hillary Clinton (Clinton Confidential, p. 455).

Wouldn't you react that way, too, if you were known as "Mrs. Bill Clinton?"

When all this is put into context...some folks are going to have a lot to answer for.

To Matt Lauer in the early days of the Lewinsky scandal (Today, 01/27/98). *During this interview she also said that "the best thing to do in these cases is just be patient, take a deep breath, and the truth will come out."*

I ran for student government president against several boys and lost, which did not surprise me, but still hurt, especially because one of [those boys] told me I was "really stupid if I thought a girl could be elected president."

A victim of a vast conspiracy even way back in high school (Living History, p. 24). *Hillary felt she lost the election because of "dirty campaigning." However, the person who defeated her told author Ed Klein the reason he won and she lost was far more basic—"I was the star running back on the football team. It was as simple as that"* (The Truth About Hillary, p. 54).

Just keep smiling until these assholes get their pictures.

Instructions to her husband while they were posing for photographers (American Evita, *p. 114*).

I don't care what other people think.

Hillary's response, early in the first term, when informed her behavior and personality had a strong negative effect on many Americans (Hillary's Choice, *p. 225*). *Gary Aldrich wrote that one White House staffer told another, "When 'Queen Hillary' walks down the hall, you're not supposed to look at her. You're actually supposed to go into an office if there is one nearby. She doesn't want staff 'seeing' her. And I know she sure as hell doesn't want to meet you or any other staffer"* (Unlimited Access, *p. 89*).

I try to be a direct person and—but I don't tell people what to do. I say, "Here's what I think and I'm concerned about this."

Hillary's response when asked if she has a temper (The Unique Voice of Hillary Rodham Clinton, *p. 81*). *Former Press Secretary Dee Dee Myers has said, "[I] think because not only would she sort of humiliate you in front of your colleagues or whoever happened to be around...Hillary tended to kind of campaign against people behind their back, and that was certainly my experience. She was not happy with me, but she never confronted me...I didn't respect that. If you have a problem with me or anybody else, it doesn't mean she shouldn't try to achieve whatever outcome she wanted to achieve. But I think there is a certain grace and I just think it's a bit better politics and personnel management to be direct"* (Frontline, *01/16/01*).

Who in the hell asked you?

Snapping at a staffer who expressed a view that she disagreed with (American Evita, *p. 125*). *A senior White House aide who worked with her on health care said, "There was a sense of self-righteousness...'I know better. I have higher standards. I have better ideals. I have bigger plans.' One gets the feeling that Hillary thinks she is better than you are"* (Hillary's Choice, *p. 241*).

I can't think of any.

Response to Dick Morris when asked to name some defects or weaknesses she could improve in order to soften her negative public image (Shadow, *p. 335).*

Woman of the People

I don't mind criticism, and I don't mind controversy, as long as people are criticizing what is being done or said instead of personally attacking each other.

(The Unique Voice of Hillary Rodham Clinton, *p. 77).*

[He] had the people skills of a porcupine.

Hillary Rodham Clinton commenting on Dick Morris's social skills (Living History, *p. 251). Hillary also wrote that Morris was "an abrasive New Yorker…who came with serious baggage."*

Hillary looking a bit prickly herself.

George Stephanopoulos getting the
short end of the stick yet again.

[He's] a traveling road show.

The World's Smartest Woman dismissing Jesse Ventura's chances of becoming the governor of Minnesota in 1998 (Showdown, p. 276).

You're a class act, Mr. Stephanopoulos.

The first lady to George Stephanopoulos, after he accepted his demotion in the Clinton White House in 1993 (All Too Human, p. 151). This is the same classy George Stephanopoulos who once referred to Phyllis Schlafly as "a far-right old-timer with a beehive hairdo" (All Too Human, p. 96).

You never believed in us...We were all alone in New Hampshire!

Circa January 1994, Hillary attacks George Stephanopoulos because he had a differing opinion on how they should deal with the growing Whitewater controversy (Frontline, 01/16/01). At this point, Stephanopoulos had dedicated two years of his life to the success of the Clintons. Dee Dee Myers said of this incident, "And anybody that stood up and tried to say this was a bad idea was, you know, smashed down and belittled, very personally. And I mean where I said the president didn't really attack people personally, Mrs. Clinton sometimes did and this was a good example" (Frontline, 01/16/01).

That is not who I am. I take care of people.

Her reaction to being criticized for allowing her staff to accumulate large legal bills regarding the reappearing billing records back in early 1996 (Washingtonpost.com, 06/14/99). One of the junior members on her White House staff said that Hillary "genuinely cared about them so long as she was convinced they were totally loyal to her and the president. If you wavered for just a sec-

ond, you were dead. Not fired. You just ceased to exist in her eyes and in her mind. We started calling it 'Hillary's Alzheimer's.' She'd be looking right at you, but you weren't there as far as she was concerned. Disloyalty—or anything that could be interpreted that way—was the one unforgivable sin" (American Evita, pp. 121-122).

I'm assuming anyone as obviously brilliant as you could find something else to market. I can't...save every under-capitalized entrepreneur in America.

The World's Smartest Woman responding to a female entrepreneur who expressed concern about losing her job due to the high costs of health care reform, circa 1993 (Newsweek 02/21/94). Hillary, who has never had to meet a payroll, then went back to calling the Republicans "the party of the rich" while claiming that the Democrats "cared about the poor."

No one thought New Jersey produced anything but concrete.

Hillary made this surprising revelation in a speech in support of New Jersey farmers (The Buffalo News, 05/19/02).

I know how tough it is in agriculture right now and I know the challenges you are up against.

Agricultural veteran Hillary Clinton on the campaign trail in upstate New York (USAToday.com, 04/26/00).

Well goddamn it Bill he's my friend, you can appoint him by law, so do it!

Hillary "advising" Governor Clinton to appoint her Rose Law Firm colleague Webb Hubbell as chief justice of the Arkansas Supreme Court, circa 1984 (Crossfire, p. 81).

Hi kiddo.

To "old friend" Lani Guinier after Hillary and Bill wouldn't support her nomination to the Justice Department once the press discovered Ms. Guinier *was insanely liberal (Hell To Pay, p. 248). After saying this, Hillary just walked on by and ignored her.*

I know the politics, I know the numbers, but it still bothers me deeply.

Hillary's comments to Dick Morris after the Clintons were forced to get rid of liberal friends and replace them with more centrist people, after the midterm elections of 1994 revealed voter backlash to their left-leaning policies (Hell To Pay, p. 285).

Damn it, that's unacceptable! Why didn't I know about this? ...[Y]ou get her on the phone!

Chastising a military aide after hearing the Clintons missed a golden PR opportunity to congratulate the woman who emulated Amelia Earhart's around the world flight (Dereliction of Duty, p. 71).

I mean, it was just an open and shut case that Abraham Lincoln was by far the greatest president, because he saved the Union and came from Illinois.

Hillary commenting on another great politician from Illinois (American Heritage" 12/94). The future senator from New York was born and raised in a suburb of Chicago, Illinois.

Celebrating Diversity

I have in the past certainly, you know maybe, called somebody a name. But I have never used an ethnic, racial, anti-Semitic, bigoted, discriminatory, prejudiced, accusation against anybody.

During the 2000 Senate campaign, responding to allegations of making an anti-Semitic remark to her husband's campaign manager after Bill's failed run for the House of Representatives in 1974 (CNN.com, 07/16/00). After this allegation came out, Hillary's staff sent a memo to her Jewish supporters urging them to come forward and state that they never heard her make an anti-

Semitic remark. The memo also stated that they should not mention they had been asked to defend her, but instead say that they were coming forward on their own because they were outraged at what was being said about her (American Evita, pp. 187-188).

She's a short, Irish bitch.

Regarding The New York Times *columnist Maureen Dowd (Newsmax.com quoting* The New York Post, 07/25/00).

Hillary: "That's all you people care about is money!"

Morris: "...I assume by 'you people,' you mean political consultants."

Hillary: "Yeah, yeah, that's what I meant, political consultants."

The first lady of Arkansas in a fight with Dick Morris, whom she knew to be Jewish, over his political consulting fee (NewsMax.com, 11/04/99).

Unlike "those people," multi-millionaire Hillary doesn't care about money at all.

"Twenty dollars on #5, please."

You fucking Jew bastard!

Honoring campaign manager Paul Fray's rich religious heritage on the night of Bill Clinton's defeat for the House of Representatives in 1974 (The State of A Union, *p. 153). Paul's wife, Mary Lee Fray, was given a special assignment during this campaign. She was to make sure that Hillary never came across "Bill's special friends" when they were campaigning around the state* (Bill & Hillary, *p. 144).*

[My] policy for the last eight years has largely been just to absorb whatever insult, charge, accusation anybody says....

After the Paul Fray "fucking Jew bastard" allegation, St. Hillary explains that she always takes the high road (USAToday.com, 07/17/00). President Clinton stated: "In 29 years my wife has never, ever, uttered an ethnic or racial slur against anybody, ever. She's so straight on this she squeaks...She can't tell an ethnic joke. It's not in her" (Hillary's Scheme, *p. 94).*

You all remember Mahatma Ghandi. He ran a gas station down in St. Louis.

Hillary during a speech at a Democratic fundraiser (CNN, 01/04/04). Senator Clinton was later forced to apologize, saying it was "a lame attempt at humor" (CNN.com, 01/07/04).

You know, I'm not going to tell that racist, sexist joke. I don't want to objectify another human being. Why do I want to do that?...Maybe I should try to restrain myself.

Telling people they should think twice before engaging in offensive behavior (New York Times Magazine, *05/23/93).*

Within and beyond their homes, adults must speak out against racial, ethnic, religious, or gender slurs.

(It Takes a Village, *p. 188*).

It did not happen. I have never said anything like that. Ever. Ever.

*Regarding her alleged racial obscenity to Paul Fray (*The Final Days, *p. 38). In August of 2000,* The New York Post *arranged to have Paul Fray take a polygraph test to verify he was telling the truth about this incident. According to a state-licensed Arkansas polygrapher, "There's no doubt in my mind that Mr. Fray is truthful" (*The New York Post, *08/22/00).*

[Violent video games] teach kids it's OK to diss people because they are a woman, they're a different color or they're from a different place.

Senator Clinton demanding a $90 million investigation into the impact of video games and other electronic media on the "cognitive, social, emotional and physical development" of children (FreeRepublic.com, 03/29/05).

If anyone thinks that one person stepping down from a leadership position cleanses the Republican Party of their constant exploitation of race, then I think you're naive.

Regarding the controversy surrounding Trent Lott when he resigned as majority leader of the Senate after stupidly praising former segregationist Strom Thurmond at his 100th birthday party (FoxNews.com, 12/20/02).

God, I'm looking in the mirror.

While waiting to testify before the Whitewater Grand Jury regarding the reappearing billing records, Hillary and her aide, Jane Sherburne, both have the same reaction of disgust and dismay that all of Ken Starr's prosecutors were white males (WashingtonPost.com 06/14/99).

Bush is advised by a [small group] of exclusively men who are, frankly, all of one mind—a very narrow, all-white [group] of exclusively men.

*Criticizing the first Bush administration because it contained too many white males (*Hillary's Choice*, p. 112). Some people might call that a slur.*

Screw them. Let's move on.

*Hillary's response when asked how the Clintons can increase their popularity with southern white males, clearly a group Hillary feels it's just fine to "diss" due to their skin color and place of origin (*Legacy*, p. 112). According to one of Hillary's top aides, "[She] is strictly a take no prisoners kind of person. The world to her is divided into two groups: our friends, and the people we want dead" (*American Evita*, p. 114).*

Motown, Motown, that's my era. Those are my people.

*The wife of America's first black president, during an interview with a Manhattan hip-hop radio station (*Newsweek*, 03/20/00).*

Hillary, attempting to groove to a Motown tune.

When you look at the way the House of Representatives has been run, it has been run like a plantation and you know what I'm talking about...

*Hillary, at a Martin Luther King Day event, in response to a question about what distinguishes Democrats from Republicans (*WCBS-TV*, 01/16/06). The Democratic senator from New York believes that her House counterparts suffer under the Republican majority in conditions not unlike those faced by*

blacks enslaved on plantations in the antebellum South. While black slaves were often beaten, malnourished, and separated from their families, House Democratic Leader Nancy Pelosi failed to disclose that she took nearly $9,000 in unforced free travel given to her by lobbyists, and her similarly enslaved House Democratic colleagues took 3,458 free trips paid by "private organizations" between 2000 and 2005 (Washington Post, 07/05/05).

I mean they're running the House of Representatives like a fiefdom with Tom DeLay as, you know, in charge of the plantation.

Hillary, in a CNN interview, again equates the House of Representatives under Republican leadership with slavery on a Southern plantation (CNN.com, 11/18/04). House Republicans would later dismiss the allegedly all-powerful DeLay as their majority leader. Since the GOP became the majority party in the House in the mid-1990s, its rules have also placed strict term limits on committee leadership positions. By contrast, Democratic committee heads, such as Energy & Commerce Committee's John Dingell (25 terms) and the Judiciary Committee's John Conyers (21 terms), can effectively hold their powerful positions for life—just like plantation masters (Chicago Sun Times, 01/05/06).

If you read about her, try not to get upset...this is a woman who truly sees the world in 19th century terms. You know, during the Clinton administration, we used to talk about building a bridge to the 21st century. This administration wants to build a bridge to the 19th century.

Regarding California Supreme Court Justice Janice Rogers Brown, a Bush nominee to the Federal Appeals court (The New York Times, 06/06/05). Evidently Justice Brown—who happens to be a black conservative—is not one of Hillary's "people."

Every time we let a religious or racial slur go unchallenged or an indignity go unanswered, we are making a choice to be indifferent...a choice, I believe, to ignore history at our children's peril.

Campaigning in New York, still ignoring allegations that she said, "you fucking Jew bastard" (NewsMax.com 07/20/00).

Who's that Quaker-looking woman over there?

Hillary making fun of a woman's looks, while at a public event in Arkansas (Crossfire, p. 85).

CHAPTER SEVEN:
Senator Clinton

The 2000 Senate Campaign

My name is Hillary Clinton. You going to vote in the primary?

Speaking to a hungry, homeless man in New York City on election day (NewsMax.com, 12/07/99). The homeless person had asked Mrs. Clinton to purchase something from him, so he could get something to eat.

Well, good for you.

Hillary's response to another homeless man when he tells her, "I'm homeless," while she was campaigning in New York City. After inquiring of his voting status, Hillary promptly left (Hannity & Colmes, 08/16/02).

"Hey, Joe, did that pushy broad ask for your vote, too?"

I wouldn't mind seeing a number of trees going to the polls on November 7th!

Regarding people who vote dressed as their favorite political issue, in the 2000 election (No Spin Zone, p. 161).

I'm not here to talk about Arkansas. I'm running in the state of New York.

Hillary's answer when asked during a debate with Rick Lazio about her education reforms while she was first lady of Arkansas (Issues2000.org, 01/21/03). Hillary's brilliant reforms and concern for the children caused Arkansas test scores to rocket from 49th all the way up to...49th.

If New Yorkers can't trust him to keep his word for ten days, how can they trust him for six years?

Lecturing her opponent, Rick Lazio, about the importance of honesty in politics and campaigns (USAToday.com, 10/09/00).

I've gone hunting. I don't have anything against guns if guns are used by responsible people...It was ducks and a long time ago.

Hillary claiming she used to go hunting while on a campaign stop in upstate New York (NewsMax.com, 06/02/02). Hunter or not, Hillary is no friend of the Second Amendment. She has been an outspoken advocate of gun control. In 2004, she voted "no" on banning lawsuits against gun manufacturers for gun violence (S1805/H.R.1036; Vote Number 2004-30, 03/02/04).

Senator Hillary

How can the Bush administration justify wanting Americans to ingest more, not less, arsenic? What's next, a "Drink Arsenic" campaign?

Press release from Senator Clinton's office about how President Bush wants to destroy the environment and poison children (Clinton.Senate.gov, 03/20/01). Even though she claimed President Bush was poisoning drinking water, she later said it was he who was "quite polarizing."

You know, we all heard about [President Bush's] charm offensive. But when it comes to the environment and public health, it sometimes appears as though his administration is on a harm offensive. Yesterday it was arsenic and about face.

Senator Clinton regarding President Bush rolling back the standards for drinking water (Clinton.Senate.gov, 03/21/01). In the ensuing five years, no deaths due to arsenic in tap water have been reported.

In breaking this promise, [President Bush] also breaks his promise to leave no child behind. Because the real victims of global warming will be our children, and their children, who will inherit an Earth suffering severe environmental consequences...

Senator Clinton hammering President Bush for opposing the Kyoto treaty (Clinton.Senate.gov, 03/14/01). Not surprisingly, Hillary neglected to note that in 1997—during her husband's presidency—the U.S. Senate voted 95-0 against implementing the Kyoto accords.

As school children distribute their hand-made Valentines in classrooms throughout America, the administration is about to announce its Valentine's Day gift to the country. Unfortunately, it's not chocolate and flowers. It's dirty air and global warming.

Another dispassionate analysis about how best to address environmental problems (Clinton.Senate.gov, 02/14/02).

[It is] one of the most activist, if not the most activist, Supreme Court ever in American history.

Senator Clinton in a speech before the liberal group the American Constitution Society about the current makeup of the U.S. Supreme Court (AP, 07/24/02). Has she ever heard of the Warren Court?

Senator Clinton thoroughly
enjoying her new job.

I like it because I have an actual job
to do, where what I'm doing is really
the most important thing to the public...If anything, the public attention
is sort of diminishing, which is fine
with me. But when it does come, it
comes because of what I'm actually
doing, and I like that.

*The ever-modest Senator Clinton ex-
plaining the difference between being
first lady and being a senator (USATo-
day.com, 07/10/01).*

[T]here's a lot more opportunity to express my own opinions, to work through
what I would do and how I would do it.

*More from HRC on being a senator
versus being first lady (Washington-
Post.com, 01/27/02).*

I have said before that I will help Democrats get elected. But there's more
of a need now because this is an election year.

*Campaigning for fellow Democrats in Iowa, in the middle of winter (The
New York Post, 02/27/02). Yogi Berra couldn't have said it better.*

I am, you know, adamantly against illegal immigrants.

*(WABC 02/03, quoted in Newsmax.com, 11/21/04). Though Hillary is one of
the few Washington politicians, of either party, to speak out against illegal
immigration, political commentator John Spencer has observed, "yet she supports an amnesty proposal that Democratic Senator Feinstein calls a 'huge
magnet' for illegal immigration" (HumanEventsOnline.com, 01/17/06).*

Hillary the Zionist

Yasser Arafat bears the responsibility for the violence that has occurred. It rests squarely on his shoulders.

Taking a tough stand against terrorism in a post-9/11 world (MidEast-Truth.com, 02/24/02).

It was a pleasure to be a part of the Massachusetts Chapter meeting of the American Muslim Alliance...The plaque is a wonderful reminder of my visit.

Hillary's thank you note, written on White House letterhead, to The American Muslim Alliance, circa June 2000 (JewishWorldReview.com, 11/06/00). The keynote speaker of this event, Stanley Cohen, said in his speech, "The true terrorists are the state of Israel and its supporter, the United States, in perpetuating the victimization of the Palestinians in their own land" (National Review Online, 11/05/00).

Hillary, friend of the Jews, embracing Suha Arafat, wife of Yasser.

I think it will be in the long-term interests of the Middle East for Palestine to be a state...

Hillary floating the idea of an independent Palestine in a speech to Arab and Israeli youths, two years before running for the Senate (AP, 05/08/98).

It must be clear that any unilateral declaration of Palestinian statehood would be entirely unacceptable...

Hillary singing a somewhat different tune with respect to Palestinian state-hood, while campaigning in New York City (USAToday.com, 07/26/00).

[You] Jew bastard...[You] Jew motherfucker.

Common insults that both Hillary and Bill Clinton used with each other and towards others who angered them, according to former bodyguard Larry Pat-terson (The State of A Union, p. 155).

[You] motherfucking Jew.

Hillary to Bill (Bitter Legacy, p. 11). On one of Hillary's first trips to Arkan-sas, she and Bill stopped by the home of one of his friends who had a menorah (a Jewish symbol) on his door. When Hillary saw this, she refused to get out of the car, causing Bill to tell his friend, "I'm sorry, but Hillary's really tight with the people in the PLO in New York. They're friends of hers, and she just doesn't feel right about the menorah...Hillary really backs the PLO and doesn't like what Israel is up to" (American Evita, p. 50).

September Eleventh

[It was] a capital offense.

Dismissing criticism of her behavior during President Bush's address to Con-gress after the September 11th attacks, when she looked bored and acted in a manner many considered disrespectful (The Washington Post, 01/27/02).

The attacks on our country were the extreme example of a hate crime.

Taking the politically courageous step of condemning the 9/11 terrorists (USAToday.com, 10/07/01). When one of Hillary's New York supporters found out that conservative commentator Barbara Olson was killed when her plane crashed into the Pentagon, he snickered, "Well, I can't say I'm sorry" (American Evita, p. 227).

The president knew what? My constituents would like to know the answer to that and many other questions, not to blame the president or any other American, just to know.

While on the floor of the Senate, Hillary holds up a New York Post *headline that proclaims, "Bush Knew," implying President Bush had advance knowledge of the terrorist attack, but let it happen (CNN.com, 05/18/02).*

Hillary's example of a "hate crime." She would later imply that President Bush had advance knowledge of the September 11th attack.

I don't know that we want to put it in a political context.

Senator Clinton objects to having Congress vote on a war resolution before the November 2002 elections (Townhall.com, 09/26/02). As Ann Coulter wrote, "Yes, it would be outrageous for politicians to have to inform the voters how they stand on important national security issues before an election" (Townhall.com, 09/26/02).

When the rest of the world opened its hearts to us [after 9/11], he turned his back and pursued a very narrow and unfortunate policy that we are still paying a very big price for.

Hillary complains about President Bush's actions in actually fighting the war on terror (Newsmax.com, 11/16/03). Hillary neglects to mention that she voted to support President Bush's narrow and unfortunate actions in Afghanistan and Iraq.

The War on Terror

I believe in evil and I think that there are evil people in the world.

Hillary's opinion of the Washington establishment and those opposed to her health care reform plan (The Agenda, p. 169). Hillary uttered this a few months after Islamic terrorists attempted to kill over 250,000 Americans in the first World Trade Center bombing in 1993.

Oh, I am well aware it is out there. One of the most difficult experiences I personally had in the White House was during the health-care debate, being the object of extraordinary rage.

Hillary's response when asked "How will Americans react realizing they are on the receiving end of murderous anger by Muslim extremists" (National Review Online, 10/03/01). Hillary is comparing the hatred of Islamic terrorists, who had murdered thousands of Americans, to that of Republicans who were opposed to her health care plan in 1993-1994. Seriously.

It's been said, and I think it's accurate, that my husband was obsessed by terrorism in general and al-Qaeda in particular.

(Dateline, 04/16/04). *In the fall of 1998, military intelligence concluded there was a two-hour window to take out bin Laden. For one hour, President Clinton could not be located. Once they did find him, the Clinton national security team debated the merits of trying to kill bin Laden. They concluded that since there was not a 100 percent guarantee of success, they wouldn't give the order* (Dereliction of Duty, *pp. 129-130).*

[I] know from personal experience—how absolutely focused [President Clinton] was on this and the kind of action that was taken.

To Tim Russert, when asked if the Clinton administration pursued Osama bin Laden, and terrorism in general, as aggressively as it should have (Meet the Press, *12/09/01). Bill Clinton's lame strike against bin Laden came in August of 1998, when Hillary was reportedly not speaking to him because of the Lewinsky scandal.*

He was "focused" and "obsessed" on something, all right.

Bill was criticized for ordering the [cruise missile] attack...by both Republicans and commentators who still didn't understand the dangers presented by terrorism in general and bin Laden and al Qaeda in particular.

Regarding the "feckless" cruise missile strike against bin Laden in August of 1998 (Living History, p. 469). Bill and Hillary forgot to get their stories straight. In his book Bill writes, "By and large, the response of the congressional leaders of both parties to the missile strikes was positive, in large part because they had been well briefed and [Secretary of Defense William Cohen] had assured his fellow Republicans that the attack and its timing were justified" (My Life, p. 450, paperback edition, vol. II). After 9/11, President Bush promised the American people, "When I take action, I'm not going to fire a $2 million missile at a $10 empty tent and hit a camel in the butt. It's going to be decisive" (Newsweek, 09/24/01).

You know, Jeff, I just don't think that's a fair assessment. You know, but I will certainly wait to, you know, learn with everyone else.

Senator Clinton's response to CNN's Jeff Greenfield when asked if Bill Clinton took the war on terror seriously enough (CNN.com, 01/17/02). You know, some people get, you know, nervous when they are, you know, lying. According to Richard Miniter, author of Losing bin Laden, *James Woolsey, President Clinton's CIA director, told him, "It wasn't that I had a bad relationship with the president. It just didn't exist" (National Review Online, 09/11/03). Furthermore, one of the reasons the U.S. didn't work with the Taliban to extradite bin Laden, according to the 9/11 Commission Report, was because "the idea might not seem attractive to either Secretary Albright or First Lady Hillary Rodham Clinton—both critics of the Taliban's record on women's rights" (The 9/11 Commission Report, p. 125).*

On paper, women had rights. They went to school, they participated in the professions...and as long as they stayed out of [Saddam's] way, they had considerable freedom of movement.

After Saddam Hussein's capture, Hillary questions whether the women of Iraq weren't better off under his rule (Newsmax.com, 02/27/04). Apparently she had never heard of Saddam's numerous rape rooms and torture chambers.

I have to admit that a good deal of what my husband and I have learned [about Islam] has come from our daughter.

Hillary addressing members of the American Muslim Council at a White House celebration of a Muslim holiday (Truthinmedia.org, 08/08/99). If President Clinton had been meeting more with his CIA Director, perhaps he wouldn't have had to rely on his teenage daughter to be his advisor on Muslim affairs. On the other hand, Democratic presidents have a history of valuing their daughters' advice on geopolitical issues. In his October 1980 debate with Ronald Reagan, Jimmy "Killer Rabbit" Carter said in response to a question on the Strategic Arms Limitation Talks: "I had a discussion with my daughter, Amy, the other day, before I came here, to ask her what the most important issue was. She said she thought nuclear weaponry — and the control of nuclear arms" (OpinionJournal.com, 06/30/04).

Foreign policy expert Chelsea Clinton leading the way.

In the four years since the inspectors left, intelligence reports show that Saddam Hussein has worked to rebuild his chemical and biological weapons stock, his missile delivery capability, and his nuclear program. He has also given aid, comfort, and sanctuary to terrorists, including al Qaeda members...[L]eft unchecked, Saddam Hussein will continue to increase his capacity to wage biological and chemical warfare, and will keep trying to develop nuclear weapons. Should he succeed in that endeavor, he could alter the political and security landscape of the Middle East, which as we know all too well affects American security.

Senator Clinton in October 2002 (Floor of the U.S. Senate, 10/10/02).

The key is to win the war. The war should not be shortchanged in any way.

To Defense Secretary Donald Rumsfeld regarding the support of Congress for the military in the war with Iraq (The Wall Street Journal, 05/06/03). William Safire has written that Hillary has gone from being "a congenital liar" to "a congenital hawk." Perhaps here's part of the reason why. According to the New York Sun, "Senators Clinton and Schumer are asking the Pentagon to spend $123 million of its wartime budget for New York projects that the Department of Defense didn't ask for—but that in many cases are linked to the senators' campaign contributors" (The New York Sun, 12/27/05).

[A]t this point in time, I think that would be a mistake. I don't believe we should tie our hands or the hands of the new Iraqi government...We don't want to send a signal to the insurgents, to the terrorists that we are going to be out of here at some, you know, certain date. I think that would be a green light to go ahead and just bide your time.

Senator Clinton rejecting an immediate withdrawal from Iraq, or the setting of a timetable for leaving Iraq (Meet the Press, 02/20/05).

If Congress had been asked [to authorize the war], based on what we know now, we never would have agreed.

Hillary in an e-mail to her constituents (NewsMax.com, 11/29/05). In the same e-mail Hillary wrote, "Criticism of this administration's policies should not in any way be confused with softness against terrorists, inadequate support for democracy or lack of patriotism." Commenting on this very nuanced stance of Hillary's, Carl Limbacher wrote, "At times…the top Democrat tried to have it both ways—trumpeting her criticism of the war while insisting she backed the troops" (NewsMax.com, 11/29/05).

I take responsibility for my vote, and I, along with a majority of Americans, expect the president and his administration to take responsibility for the false assurances, faulty evidence and mismanagement of the war.

Senator Clinton, in the same e-mail to her constituents (Newsmax, 11/29/05). "I have ordered a strong, sustained series of air strikes against Iraq. They are designed to degrade Saddam's capacity to develop and deliver weapons of mass destruction, and to degrade his ability to threaten his neighbors…The best way to end that threat once and for all is with a new Iraqi government—a government ready to live in peace with its neighbors, a government that respects the rights of its people" (President Clinton, explaining to the nation his decision to authorize airstrikes against Iraq, 12/16/98).

You know, I believe that you can be very tough, you can enforce America's interests and values while still talking.

Senator Clinton criticizing President Bush for his tough stance in dealing with North Korea (ABC Radio News, 12/27/02). The Bush administration had stopped negotiating with North Korea because that country had violated an agreement with the U.S. not to pursue a nuclear weapons program. President Jimmy Carter had negotiated the agreement in 1994 for the Clinton administration.

Put simply, they couldn't do that when George Bush became president, and now they can.

Senator Clinton's reaction to news that North Korea now has the ability to arm a missile with a nuclear device that can reach the United States (The New York Times, 04/29/05). However, she neglected to mention that it was her husband who supplied them with the technology.

Well, you know, Tim, I don't think that you either rule it in or rule it out. I think that, you know, depending upon circumstances, it's something that, you know, the American government would have to, you know, consider.

Her response to a question regarding using military force with Iran (Meet the Press, 02/20/05). Ah...you know...well...thanks for the, you know, definitive answer, Senator Clinton.

President Hillary

Better make up your mind Bill, if you don't run, I will.

Urging her husband to run for president in 1992 (Bill & Hillary, p. 226).

Coming to an Oval Office near you?

Not that I can imagine. No, that is not anything I have ever thought of for myself...

In 1997 Hillary is asked if she would ever consider running for political office at some point in the future (Larry King Live, 04/29/97). Even during the impeachment hearings, she had her eye on the New York Senate seat. Said one party official, "We all knew she wanted it so bad she could taste it. But she knew it would never happen if President Clinton was run out of office in disgrace" (American Evita, p. 173).

Right now I don't know if he has a future, but I intend to.

Circa August 1998, just after Bill confessed to suborning perjury about his indiscretions with Monica Lewinsky to the nation, Hillary expressed concern for her political future (American Evita, *p. 170*).

I want independence. I want to be judged on my own merits.

Her reaction to always being thought of as just the wife of a politician (Talk Magazine, *08/99*).

People think that because I care so much about public issues, I should run for office myself. I don't want to run for office.

(The Unique Voice of Hillary Rodham Clinton, *p. 63*).

Eight years of Bill, eight years of Hill. That was the plan.

Hillary telling a friend of their plans for the presidency, shortly after arriving in the White House in January 1993 (Hillary's Scheme, *p. 18*). *A White House staff member said, "There was a lot of talk about 'The Plan.' [Bill & Hillary] joked around about it in a cloak-and-dagger way, but you could tell they were serious"* (American Evita, *p. 155*).

People have said that to me, but it is something I don't take seriously…

Response when asked if she'd ever run for president (Hell to Pay, *p. 13*).

Eight years of Hill, baby.

We'll have a woman president by 2010.

When asked if she'd ever run for the presidency, circa the 1992 campaign (The Unique Voice of Hillary Rodham Clinton, *p. 64*).

I want to run something.

A frustrated Hillary to a friend, after her health care plan failed in Congress (Hillary's Choice, *p. 226*).

I think our country should have a woman president within a short period of time, I've been saying that for many years.

(Katv.com, 05/24/04). One wonders whom she has in mind?

I have said that I'm not running and I'm having a great time being pres——being a first-term senator...[Y]ou guys are going to get me into a lot of trouble.

The crowd laughed nervously at this Freudian slip by Hillary during a speech at the National Press Club (Newsmax.com, 07/19/01).

You know, Tim, I have no intention of running for president.

(Meet the Press, 12/9/01).

TIM RUSSERT: "Would you accept the nomination [in 2004] for president or vice president?"

HILLARY CLINTON: "No."

RUSSERT: "Will you run in 2008?"

HILLARY: "I have no plans to run for president."

(Meet the Press, 09/15/02). Bernadette Chirac, wife of French President Jacques Chirac has said of Hillary, "A lot of women hope that one day she will run for the presidency of the United States, and that she'll win." When a reporter from the German magazine Bunte *remarked that "some people" were*

disappointed she wasn't running in 2004, she replied, "I know. Well, perhaps I'll do it next time around" (American Evita, p. 257).

Sounds good.

Her reaction to a man yelling to her, "President Clinton!" while campaigning for Senator in New York (Hillary Clinton's Plans for the Presidency, p. 3).

CHAPTER EIGHT:
Hillary the Socialist

I just feel that Hillary is a socialist, and I'm paying enough tax. Hillary wants to take my money, [and] your money…and give it to strangers. There's something about that that offends me.

—Bill O'Reilly to Jay Leno (*The Tonight Show*, 05/20/02)

It's Her World—You're Just Infesting It

See how liberal I'm becoming!

From coed Hillary Rodham's letter to a friend about her transformation from Republican/Goldwater girl to liberal Democrat (Hell to Pay, p. 35). She also said, "I'm a heart liberal, but a mind conservative" (Hillary's Choice, p. 83).

Hillary, getting in touch with her inner liberal.

The basic rationale for depriving people of rights...is that certain individuals are incapable or undeserving of the right to take care of themselves and consequently need social institutions specifically designed to safeguard their position. Along with the family, past and present examples of such arrangements include marriage, slavery, and the Indian reservation system.

Hillary's views on marriage are spelled out in an article from the early 1970s (Harvard Educational Review, *November 1973, quoted in* Hell to Pay, *p. 107). Former Yale law professor Judge Robert Bork has said regarding Bill and Hillary Clinton, "Both the man from Hope and Hillary were students of mine when I taught at the Yale Law School. Well, I no longer say they were my students. I say they were in the room...some of the time" (AEI.org, 02/13/01).*

Too many women are asking what good is democracy when we don't have affordable child care or health care. Too many workers are asking what good is a free market when we are the first to be fired and the last to be hired.

Hillary criticizes democracy and the free market while on a European trip (BBC News Online Network, 10/10/99). "Asking liberals where wages and prices come from is like asking six-year-olds where babies come from"— Thomas Sowell (Libertarianquotes.com, 01/12/06).

Decisions about motherhood and abortion, schooling, cosmetic surgery, treatment of venereal disease, or employment, [which] will significantly affect the child's future, should not be made unilaterally by parents.

*Hillary the multi-lateralist expressing her views on parental rights in a 1978 essay, "Children's Rights: A Legal Perspective" (*Hell to Pay, *p. 110).*

It's time to put the common good, the national interest, ahead of individuals.

Soon-to-be-multi-millionaire Hillary Clinton's response when a woman complained that she didn't want to be forced into a health care plan she didn't like (JewishWorldReview.com, 07/08/99).

We are at a stage in history in which remolding society is one of the great challenges facing all of us in the West.

Hillary stating her goal of reshaping America, whether it likes it or not, in a 1993 commencement speech at the University of Texas (Hell to Pay, p. 310).

As a society, we have a choice to make. We can permit the marketplace largely to determine the values and well-being of the village, or we can continue...to expect business to play a social as well as an economic role.

More economic wisdom from a lawyer and politician who never had to make a payroll (It Takes a Village, p. 297). In 1993, former Democratic Senator and presidential candidate George McGovern said of his late-in-life foray into the business world that being the owner of a business was a "punishingly revelatory experience." He wrote: "I'm not expert enough after only two and a half years as a business owner to know the solutions to all those concerns. I do know that if I were back in the U.S. Senate or in the White House, I would ask a lot of questions before I voted for any more burdens on the thousands of struggling businesses across the nation" (Inc. Magazine, 12/93).

The unfettered free market has been the most radically disruptive force in American life in the last generation.

Former corporate attorney and Wal-Mart board member, multi-millionaire, and current Georgetown resident Hillary Clinton on the evils of capitalism (Booknotes, 03/03/96). Contrast this to Ronald Reagan's view of the free market: "Millions of individuals making their own decisions in the marketplace will always allocate resources better than any centralized government planning process" (RonaldReagan.com, 01/12/06).

Other developed countries...are more committed to social stability than we have been, and they tailor their economic policies to maintain it.

(It Takes a Village, p. 296). For example, take France: "French unemployment has hovered around 10 percent for years...France's tax burden is one of the highest in Europe—welfare states don't come cheap. The top marginal

income tax rate is 48 percent. When payroll taxes are included, the French can pay as much as 65 percent of their income in taxes. The top corporate tax rate is 34 percent. There is also a 19.6 percent value-added tax (VAT). Overall, taxes consume nearly 44 percent of France's GDP. And even this isn't enough to pay for the French welfare state. France's national debt tops 68 percent of GDP, quite aside from the unfunded liabilities of the French Social Security system—a debt some estimate to exceed 200 percent of GDP" (The Washington Times, *11/15/05).*

[Republicans] don't just want to roll back on Bill Clinton's policies. They're working on Franklin Roosevelt's and Teddy Roosevelt's as well.

While campaigning on behalf of Governor Gray Davis in California, Senator Clinton explained that any tax cut or reduction in government will take America back to the Dark Ages (NewsMax.com, 10/06/02). Just months later, Hillary's candidate was recalled by the voters of California, in part for being an economic incompetent.

HILLARY: "If you tinker with one part of this system, you screw the whole thing up. You've got to deal with all of it or leave it alone."

DICK MORRIS: "You sound like a goddamned Stalinist!...Give me a break."

An argument over accepting a compromise with the Republicans related to her health care plan, circa 1994 (Hillary's Choice, p. 251). When he realized that the Clintons were not governing as the "centrist Democrats" that they had campaigned as, an exasperated Dick Morris asked James Carville, "What's with all this liberalism?" Carville responded, "These fucking liberals are all over the place! They are like water damage. They seep in" (Hillary's Choice, p. 231).

This whole budget and tax cut plan puts politics first and people last. We're in for a fight—I intend to be on the front lines of that fight.

Senator Clinton demonstrating that she opposed any kind of plan that let the taxpayers keep more of their own money (Let Freedom Ring, p. 220).

We must stop thinking of the individual and start thinking about what is best for society.

The first lady in 1993 (WorldNetDaily.com, 10/01/02).

Many of you are well enough off that [President Bush's] tax cuts may have helped you. We're saying that for America to get back on track, we're probably going to cut that short and not give it to you. We're going to take things away from you on behalf of the common good.

(SFGate.com, 06/28/04). Although she was speaking to wealthy donors, nothing illustrates Hillary's truest and most sincerely held beliefs better than this quote. Fortunately for Hillary, she can afford good tax advice. "Although she now praises the tax code as an instrument of social equity, Hillary has made full use of available means to minimize her 'contribution.' A tax accountant familiar with her returns told investigative journalist Daniel Wattenberg that 'she's always made out like a bandit'" (TheNewAmerican.com, 07/12/93).

Nikita Khrushchev once said, "We must abolish the cult of the individual, once and for all."

I'm a new Democrat. I don't believe government is the source of all of our problems or the solution to them.

Announcing her candidacy for senator (Issues2000.org, 02/06/00).

Hillary the Macro-Economist

We didn't come here to spend all our time cutting deficits created by Republicans.

Regarding Bill Clinton's broken promise to cut taxes for the middle class (Eyewitness to Power, p. 277). The Clinton team instead hit the public with a record tax increase. The massive hike barely garnered Congressional approval, requiring Al Gore's tie-breaking vote in the Senate.

The [Bush] administration has begun to destroy in less than eight months what it took our nation, on a bipartisan basis, eight years to achieve. If this were a movie, it would be called *Honey, I Shrunk The Surplus.*

Attacking Bush's 2001 tax cuts (Clinton.Senate.gov, 09/05/01). Most economists now agree that the tax cuts lessened the severity of the 2001 recession, and that Bush's follow-up round of cuts in 2003 spurred the post-9/11 economy back to life.

They have the most wrong-headed economic policies that we've seen since Herbert Hoover and we're beginning to pay a price as a nation for these policies.

Criticizing President Bush's tax cuts (Hannity & Colmes, 04/29/03). "Since May 2003—which not coincidentally was the debut period for Bush's tax cuts on personal income, dividends, and capital gains—the economy has generated 3 million new jobs. Using the Labor Department's household survey, 2.6 million more people have been employed since the tax cuts. The unemployment rate has dropped to 5.4 percent from 6.3 percent. Weekly unemployment claims have fallen to 300,700—the lowest since late 2000" (National Review Online, 03/04/05).

We've seen this before. This is what was done in the 1980s and it took about eight years to get out of the deficit ditch and to get a surplus so that we could be prepared for rainy days and even terrible tragedies like what happened to us on 9/11.

Criticizing the Reagan tax cuts for the huge deficits in the 1980s, but ignoring the spending increases made by the Democrats who controlled Congress (Newsmax.com, 09/05/02). Perhaps with Hillary in mind, President Reagan once quipped, "It isn't that liberals are ignorant. It's just that they know so much that isn't so" (Wikiquote.com, 01/12/06).

You know, I'm a big fan of Clintonomics, and this administration is destroying in months our eight years of economic progress.

Attacking President Bush while at a fundraiser in Los Angeles (MSNBC.com, 10/28/02). Perhaps Hillary should read "Why U.S. Economic Growth is Galloping" (BusinessWeekOnline.com, 12/08/05).

Today, New York has the largest gap between the rich and the poor of any state in the United States. Therefore it is time for our friends in the rest of the country to return the favor and to change the way business is done in Washington to give New York its fair share.

Demanding that more money go to New York for social programs (CNN, 02/07/00). Immediately after 9/11, Hillary and Senator Schumer successfully wrangled $21.4 billion for New York from the federal government. However, a four-month investigation by New York's Daily News revealed that the process for doling out the $21.4 billion disaster recovery package was "procedurally flawed—and that there was little oversight [over the spending]." The News went on to report, "In effect, no one was watching, including Mrs. Clinton" (NewsMax.com, 12/04/05).

Getting a high score from this group would mean cutting billions of dollars in aid for New York.

Hillary's reaction to getting an F grade (for her 3 percent rating), the lowest rating ever for a freshman senator, from the National Taxpayers Union, a group that monitors the biggest tax-and-spenders in Congress (News-Max.com, 03/28/02).

The Bush economic plan turns [Churchill's] saying on its head: Never in the field of economics have so few been given so much at the expense of so many.

Multi-millionaire Senator Hillary Clinton criticizes President Bush's "tax cuts for the rich" tax plan, during a speech on the floor of the Senate on 01/09/03 (Clinton.Senate.gov).

[It] is a lifeline for many individuals already struggling to make ends meet. And now the president wants to leave them out in the cold.

Regarding President Bush's plans to reduce federal aid for 154 government programs, including the Community Development Block Grant Program to which Hillary refers here (CAGW.org, 02/15/05). Citizens Against Government Waste jointly named Clinton and Schumer "Porker of the Month" for February 2005 for opposing these reductions, which saved U.S. taxpayers $15 billion (CAGW.org, 02/15/05).

I have been consistent in my commitment to maintaining fiscal responsibility...I believe in affordable tax cuts. I would like to see some tax cuts.

Hillary claiming to be in favor of tax cuts, while criticizing President Bush's plan to cut taxes (Clinton.Senate.gov, 02/05/01).

If we hadn't passed the big tax cut last spring, that I believe undermined our fiscal responsibility and our ability to deal with this new threat of terrorism, we wouldn't be in the fix we're in today.

Just days before the liberation of Afghanistan from the Taliban regime, Senator Clinton explains how Bush's tax cuts left the United States vulnerable to the 9/11 attacks, and how they are to blame for our inability to defeat the terrorists in that country (CNN.com, 11/11/01).

When I read today's *Washington Post* article about the administration's plans to increase the tax burden on low-income workers, I had to check the date and make sure that it wasn't April Fool's Day.

Accusing the evil Republicans of raising taxes on the poor, while giving tax breaks to the rich like herself (Clinton.Senate.gov, 12/16/02). Which might not be a bad thing if it prevents Hillary from donating Bill's used underwear to charity for the tax break.

I consider [right-wing talk radio] my gift to the American economy. I mean, think of all the people who have made a living...with the sole purpose and obsession, I guess, of talking about and writing about me.

(Talkers Magazine, 09/04).

The Arctic Refuge is part of what makes our country so unique, so beautiful, and so precious. It deserves protection, not exploitation.

Fighting to protect the Alaskan wilderness from the greedy Republicans, and their friends in "Big Oil" (Let Freedom Ring, p. 190).

Put simply, the oil companies get to drill, while the American people foot the bill.

Doing her best to imitate Jesse Jackson, while criticizing President Bush's energy policies (Clinton.Senate.gov, 05/17-/01). Domestic oil drilling is likely opposed by Saudi Arabia, whose business elite donated millions to build her husband's library.

Reports of Hillary giving President Bush and his economic advisers a bronx cheer may not have been exaggerated afterall.

They're more interested in tax cuts for the rich than for flu shots for everyone who needs them.

Blasting the Republicans for the mythical flu vaccine shortage (Newsmax.com, 10/18/04). One of her Senate colleagues said about working with her, "She says nice things, but you get the sense that she hates you...Her every action betrays a deep-seated hatred of conservatism." An aide to another senator said, "Underneath it all, I believe she regards anyone who disagrees with her as an enemy and a fool" (Madame Hillary, p. 44).

Hillary the Micro-Economist

Too many people have made too much money.

Regarding the greedy people in the health care industry (TheNewAmerican.com, 07/13/93). Years later Hillary would accept $8 million for her memoirs, while her husband would accept $12 million for his.

I am pleased that the Senate Ethics Committee has found that my agreement with Simon & Schuster fully complies with the Senate ethics rules.

Regarding her $8 million book deal (USAToday.com, 02/14/01). When Newt Gingrich signed his book deal for $4.5 million in 1994, he was widely condemned by the Democrats for his greed. Bill Clinton said about Gingrich, "I don't even know how to think in those terms" (JewishWorldReview.com, 12/28/00). He and Hillary apparently caught on fast.

We're the party of the people, and they're the party of the rich and the special interests—it's really that simple.

Multi-millionaire Hillary attacking George W. Bush and Dick Cheney during the 2004 campaign (American Evita, p. 245). An old friend of hers says, "I watched Hillary turn the world into Us versus Them. That's how she looks at the world: she and Bill are good people with the grandest intentions who keep getting screwed" (Hillary's Choice, p. 146). While in Arkansas during Reagan's "decade of greed," "party of the people" person Hillary served on three corporate boards, including that of Wal-Mart, and made handsome fees as a corporate attorney.

Life is too short to spend it making money for some big anonymous firm.

Future Rose Law Firm partner and Wal-Mart board member Hillary Rodham's early view of life (The Great Whitewater Fiasco, *p. 34*).

Throughout the 1980s, we heard too much about individual gain, about the ethos of selfishness and greed. We did not hear enough about what it meant to be a member of a community.

Hillary condemning the greed of the business world of the 1980s, but neglecting to mention that during the same period she was a well-paid corporate attorney who served on the boards of Wal-Mart, the TCBY yogurt company, and the French chemical firm La Farge (TheNewAmerican.com, 07/12/93).

While Hillary's disdain for capitalism did not stop her from inking an $8 million book deal, she's "keeping the faith" by wearing what looks to be a Chairman Mao jacket from the late 1960s.

You're getting your ass out there, and you're doing what has to be done.

"Advising" President Clinton during the 1996 re-election campaign when he complained he was tired of all the fundraising (American Evita, *p. 150*).

To Johnny Chung, with best wishes and appreciation.

*Hillary's thank you note to Chung, who was a major figure in the 1996 fundraising scandal (VillageVoice.com, 08/10/99). Regarding the $50,000 he gave to Hillary's top aide in order to receive VIP treatment from the Clintons, Mr. Chung said, "I see the White House is like a subway—you have to put in coins to open the gates."(*The News Hour, *08/22/99). Yet both Clintons regularly bemoan the influence of money in politics.*

That's just right-wing bullshit.

Dismissing criticism from Republicans complaining about the illegal fundraising activities of the Democrats during the 1996 presidential campaign (American Evita, *p. 152*). *Oftentimes when criticized, President Clinton would say he wasn't concerned with the allegations, but instead he would "get back to work for the American people." However, during the 1996 fundraising season he complained to Dick Morris, "I haven't slept in three days; every time I turn around they want me to be at a fundraiser…I cannot think, I cannot do anything. Every minute of my time is spent at these fundraisers"* (Absolute Power, *p. 171*).

What the [expletive] did we come here for? There's no money here!

Furious at one of her staffers, because a political rally being held on a dairy farm in upstate New York lacked big money donors (A Matter of Character, *p. 3*). *If there were sparse crowds when she made an appearance during the Senate campaign, "[She] flew into rages when she thought her campaign staff had not corralled enough onlookers beforehand. Hillary had an explosive temper"* (A Matter of Character, *p. 2*).

You need to send us money. We need it now, and we need all you can send.

Hillary, wife to a selfless public servant, makes a desperate plea for money during a phone call to Jim McDougal, the morning after "their" defeat in the 1980 gubernatorial election (Blood Sport, p. 97).

CHAPTER NINE:
Hillary Miscellany

Champion of the First Amendment

We're all going to have to rethink how we deal with the Internet. As exciting as these new developments are, there are a number of serious issues without any kind of editing function or gatekeeping function.

On the disturbing trend of free speech on the Internet (Sfgate.com, 02/22/98).

It is just beyond imagination what can be disseminated...[I] don't have any clue about what we're going to do legally, regulatory, technologically...we're going to have to deal with that.

In an appearance just weeks after Matt Drudge posted the Monica Lewinsky story on his website, the first lady stresses that action is needed regarding the issue of free speech and the Internet (DrudgeReportArchives.com, 02/12/98).

People Who Boo Hillary

Thank you, thank you for being here...

Mrs. Clinton struggles to be heard over the boos at a benefit concert for New York City cops and firemen (News-Max.com, 10/22/01). Firefighter Mike Moran, who lost a brother to 9/11, explained the reaction. "I think when times are good...people will sit there and listen to the kind of claptrap that comes out of her mouth. When things are like this, when it's serious times and serious men who actually suffered losses, and she wants to spew her nonsense ..." (Rush Limbaugh, 10/23/01).

You found *what* on the Internet? Call Al.
He invented it; maybe he can shut it down.

They [the firefighters and police] can blow off steam any way they want to, they've earned it.

Her response when asked about being booed off the stage at the benefit concert (The New York Times Magazine, 12/16/01). *The policemen may have remembered a spitting incident during the 2000 New York State Democratic Convention. While the Albany Police honor guard marched past a crowd of Hillary supporters, they were spit on and called "Nazis" by some official Democratic delegates. In a semi-apology, Hillary told Albany Mayor Jerry Jennings that she was appalled by the coverage of the incident, but didn't apologize for the incident itself* (WorldNetDaily.com, 01/18/06).

I've gotten used to being in situations in political life, either vicariously or on my own, where that just happens sometimes.

Regarding being booed at public events—in her mind, for no apparent reason (The New York Times Magazine, 12/16/01).

It's not really about me. I find it hard to take a lot of that personally, since the portrait is a distorted, inaccurate one.

Another comment regarding why so many people dislike her (The Unique Voice of Hillary Rodham Clinton, p. 60.)

I know I'm the projection for many of those wounded men. I'm the boss they never wanted to have. I'm the wife who went to school and got an extra degree and a job as good as theirs. I'm the daughter who they never wanted to turn out to be so independent. It's not me personally, they hate—it's the changes I represent.

Another self-congratulatory explanation as to why she is so unpopular with men (Legacy, p. 111). *Dick Morris offered the following explanation for this type of thinking on Hillary's part: "When Hillary is attacked, she frequently parries the charges by arguing that it is all women who are under attack, rather than just one in particular"* (Rewriting History, p. 57). *When Hillary was initially denied a speaking platform at the 2004 Democratic convention,*

Judith Hope, a major backer of Hillary, said of the slight, "It's a slap in the face...for every woman in the Democratic Party, and every woman in America" (The Washington Times, 07/15/04).

A Vast Turtle Conspiracy?!?

One of my husband's favorite old Southern sayings...is that if you find a turtle on a fence post, it didn't get there by accident. And I just look at the landscape around here and I see lots of big old turtles sitting on lots of fence posts. I think we need to find out how those turtles got on those fence posts.

Hillary the inscrutable, in an interview in the early days of the Lewinsky scandal (Good Morning America, 01/28/98).

Want to know how I got on that fence, lady? Your husband put me there.

[The Swiftboat ads] are not only unfair, they're flat-out wrong...[C]ertainly people close to [President Bush's] campaign have been involved with them. If you find a turtle on a fence post, you know it didn't get there by accident.

Regarding the ads by the group Swiftboat Veterans for Truth, which criticized John Kerry's service in Vietnam and may have ultimately torpedoed his presidential bid (Federalist.com, 09/08/04).

One of the great victories of the 1990s is that we drove the crime rate down and you know what? It didn't happen by accident...if you find a turtle on a fence post, it didn't get there by accident. Well if you drive the crime rate down to the lowest levels in thirty years, it didn't happen by accident.

Hillary lauding her co-presidency's crime-fighting success (DLC.org, 07/29/02). Of course, the same "turtle on a fence post" logic could be applied to Whitewater, the billing records, Travelgate, Juanita Broaddrick, the cattle futures, Filegate, the Lincoln Bedroom, the loss of missile secrets to the Chinese, Kathleen Willey, impeachment, Presidential Library donations, the pardons, the missing Ws...

I've Always Been a Yankees Fan

Being a [Chicago] Cubs fan prepares you for life—and Washington.

(Newsweek, 04/18/94).

The fact of the matter is, I've always been a Yankees fan. I am a Cubs fan, but I needed an American League team...so as a young girl, I became very interested and enamored of the Yankees.

To Katie Couric, after Ms. Couric observed Hillary wearing a Yankees hat just as she started her race for the Senate (The Today Show, 06/10/99). A short time later, during a ceremony honoring him for pitching a perfect game, then-Yankees pitcher David Cone humorously took the opportunity to slam Hillary by telling actual Yankees fan Mayor Rudy Giuliani, "I'd like to say on behalf of all the Yankee players that your sincerity as a Yankee fan really comes across. I mean there's a lot of politicians who say they are baseball fans and put on the cap…" (The First Partner, *p. 416*).

I've always been a Patrick Ewing fan because you know he went to Georgetown.

More to Katie Couric about her sudden interest in New York athletics; this time, about the legendary Knicks center (The Today Show, *06/10/99*).

I know and you know that Chicago is my kind of town. And Chicago is my kind of village.

The future Senator from New York, and "life-long Yankees fan," at the 1996 Democrat Convention, held in Chicago (CNN, *08/27/96*).

I've told a lot of people over the years that after the White House years I wanted to move to New York and have a chance to experience New York City and everything that goes with it.

During the Senate race in 2000, her response when asked about her move to New York (Larry King Live, *08/14/00*).

Lord, please let the Cubs play the Yankees in the World Series this fall.
(We just want to see her wear both hats at once.)

Hillary's Hair

I know that there are people who have very strong negative feelings towards me...It's personal, they don't like my hairstyle, they don't like my outspokenness.

(BBC Radio4, 07/07/03). That is why she is so unpopular with Republicans. It's not because she says Republicans want to starve children and poison the environment. It's because they don't like her hair.

If I want to knock a story off the front page, I just change my hairstyle.

Hillary explaining how much power she and her latest hairstyle have to shape the headlines (BrainyQuotes.com, 01/16/06).

Mrs. Clinton's Hairstyles

JAN. 93   MARCH 93   MAY 93   JUNE 93   SEPT. 93

FEB. 94   APRIL 94   APRIL 94   NOV. 94   NOV. 94

I'm undaunted in my quest to amuse myself by constantly changing my hair.

(*BrainyQuotes.com 01/16/06*). *When giving a speech on the subject of hard choices, Hillary also remarked, "Then I got to Washington and I learned the hard choices were hairstyles"* (Hillary's Choice, *p. 244*).

Guy, you son of a bitch.

Joking with Arkansas friend Guy Campbell when he tells her, "You actually resemble a beautiful woman," circa 1982 (Bill & Hillary, *p. 186*). *After Clinton was defeated in the 1980 gubernatorial election, the Clintons were informed that many Arkansans didn't like Hillary's 1960s hippy appearance. By 1982 she had gotten a complete makeover.*

Strange Bedfellows

[The Contract with America] came to be known around the White House as the "Contract on America" because of the damage it would cause our country.

(Living History, *pp. 249-50*). *Some of these "damaging" items from the "Contract with America" found in the Republican Contract With America section of the House website were: 1) "require all laws that apply to the rest of the country also apply equally to the Congress"; 2) require the selection of "a major, independent auditing firm to conduct a comprehensive audit of Congress for waste, fraud or abuse"; and 3) "require committee meetings to be open to the public"* (House.gov, *01/25/06*).

I know it's a bit of an odd-fellow, or odd-woman, mix. But the speaker and I have been talking about health care and national security now for several years, and I find that he and I have a lot in common...

On working with Newt Gingrich (The New York Times, *05/13/05*). *A senior Democratic strategist said, "By trotting her out with some Republican every other week, it shows she's not the crazy liberal you think she is. But it also conveys that she'll do anything to get elected"*(LATimes.com, *08/08/05*).

I'm afraid they'll clone Strom Thurmond and he'll be around forever.

Hillary's response when asked about cloning (The New York Post, 12/13/01).

When Her Mouth's Moving, She's Lying

Why do I keep having to prove to people that I am not a liar?

Regarding allegations of her shockingly anti-semitic comment to Paul Fray (The Survivor, p. 382). *According to the Federal Bureau of Investigation, the best indicator of future behavior is past behavior.*

I've always been a praying person.

Addressing a group of religious leaders (The Boston Globe, 01/20/05). *Hillary made this announcement soon after the 2004 election, where many voters said that the religious faith of President George W. Bush was the most important issue for them.*

"I could never tell a lie."

So when I was born, she called me Hillary, and she always told me it's because of Sir Edmund Hillary.

First Lady Hillary Clinton explaining that she was named after famous explorer, Sir Edmund Hillary (The New York Times, 04/03/95). *Only problem—Hillary Rodham was born five years before Edmund Hillary became famous by scaling Mt. Everest in 1953. The year she was born, Edmund Hillary was an obscure beekeeper in New Zealand* (Rewriting History, p. 11).

[Chelsea had] gone on what she thought would be a great jog...[S]he was going to go around the towers. She went to get a cup of coffee and that's when the plane hit...She did hear it. She did.

Hillary explaining to Jane Pauley that Chelsea was close enough to the World Trade Center on the morning of 9/11 to actually hear the impact of the first plane and that she was in potential danger (Dateline, 09/17/01). *Chelsea later wrote a first-person account of her experience on 9/11 for* Talk *magazine. Her version contradicted her mother's story from* Dateline. *Chelsea wrote she was in a friend's apartment on the other side of town and watched the horrific events of that day unfold on television. She did not mention a jog around the towers or getting coffee when the planes hit* (Talk, 11/09/01).

I spent most of my time working for [an attorney] researching, writing legal motions and briefs for a child custody case.

Writing in her autobiography what she did while an intern at the Oakland, California, law firm of Treuhaft, Walker, and Burnstein, summer of 1971 (Living History, p. 55). *Hillary actually worked on Black Panther cases, including the famous incident where the Panthers entered the State Legislature in Sacramento carrying guns. According to one of the firm's partners, "Anyone who went to college or law school would have known our law firm was a Communist firm...The biggest things we had that summer were Panther cases...Hillary went with me when I met the Sacramento County DA's office. She had done intelligent research for me and seemed interested in the whole thing. She certainly expressed no distaste for what we were doing...We pleaded it and got everything knocked down to minor charges"* (Hillary's Choice, pp. 80-82).

I have gone from a Barry Goldwater Republican to a New Democrat, but I think my underlying values have remained pretty constant; individual responsibility and community.

(NewYorkMagazine.com 04/03/00). Readers who skipped Chapter Eight are advised to read it now in order to properly evaluate this claim.

Even at that early stage, I was against all these people who came up with these big government programs that were more supportive of bureaucracies than they were actually helpful to people...

Hillary explaining the principles that caused her to work for Republicans in the 1960s, and how, in her mind, her activities as a liberal Democrat today remain true to those same principles (The Unique Voice of Hillary Rodham Clinton, *p. 59). Can you say health care reform?*

I find it so amusing when people think I'm in favor of big government, or big anything, because I'm not.

(Hell to Pay, p. 259, quoting Parade *magazine).*

Three Refreshingly Clinton-Free Campaigns

Sure, like this guy is smart enough
to set anyone up.

[They] set Bill up.

Hillary felt the Dukakis people were responsible for the disastrous introduction speech that Clinton gave at the 1988 Democrat Convention (Friends in High Places, *p. 144). This "introduction speech" dragged on for over thirty minutes and was widely ridiculed.*

It was one of the most agonizing moments of my life because I knew that we had been misled...

The World's Smartest Woman trying to understand why the Dukakis people would sabotage Bill's introduction speech (The First Partner, *p. 187).*

I can't wait to watch Al Gore take the oath of office on January 20th, 2001. Standing next to him will be his wonderful wife and my dear friend [Tipper].

At the 2000 Democratic convention (Online Newshour, 08/14/00). When Al Gore endorsed Howard "The Scream" Dean in the 2004 Democratic primaries, a New York State party official reported that Hillary said Gore was "an ungrateful putz" (American Evita, p. 261).

I'm going to be her most enthusiastic supporter because I think she'd be terrific.

Hillary endorsing the idea of her "dear friend" Tipper running for the U.S. Senate (NewsMax.com, 03/15/02). Privately, however, aides to Senator Clinton said that Hillary really believed that, "Tipper is an un-intellectual, nice lady who doesn't have a brain in her head" (OpinionJournal.com, 06/05/01).

Hillary yukking it up with "dear friend" Tipper.

The candidates we have in this campaign are...the most accomplished, in terms of public service, that we've had since 1960. One of them will be successful.

Regarding the chances of the Democrats to defeat President George W. Bush in 2004 (PoliticsUS.com, 11/21/03). One wonders what the "ungrateful putz" thought of this remark.

I'm delighted he's going to be president. He's the perfect man for this moment, a serious man for a serious time.

Commenting on John Kerry's 2004 presidential campaign (Newsmax.com, 07/25/04). A Boston politico, who had known John Kerry for over twenty-five years, said, "John doubted she'd jump in [the 2004 race], but he sure as hell knew she didn't want another Democrat to beat Bush, no matter what she said" (American Evita, p. 255).

Yup. A "serious man for a serious time," all right.

I was very disappointed...I did everything I could to help him.

To Larry King after John Kerry was defeated in the 2004 presidential race, an outcome which cleared the way for her to run in 2008 (Larry King Live, 11/17/04). Crocodile Tears, noun: a hypocritical display of sorrow; false or insincere weeping.

CHAPTER TEN

The Company She Keeps

Hillary's Friends, Cronies, and Fellow Travelers in Their Own Words

Slick Willie

You know, they just don't like her hair.

Bill Clinton during the 1992 campaign, attempting to explain why so many people in a focus group had such an intense, negative reaction upon seeing Hillary's picture (All's Fair, p. 174).

I don't know when we can get together again. "The Warden" doesn't let me out too often.

Circa 1974, Bill whining to one of his paramours about his fiancée, Hillary Rodham (Bill & Hillary, p. 131).

You better put some ice on that.

Bill Clinton to Juanita Broaddrick about her swollen lip, just moments after raping her in a Little Rock hotel in 1978 (The Wall Street Journal, 02/19/99).

What's all the fuss about; it was just a goddamn mother-fucking pig.

Governor Bill Clinton's reaction upon seeing all the people at a funeral for a black state trooper killed in the line of duty, as retold by former bodyguard Larry Patterson during an audiotape interview with Newsmax (Newsmax

Bill Clinton oozing sincerity.

Media, 2002). The future "First Black President" later apologized, but only after being chastised by his security guards (Newsmax Media, 2002).

Yes, the president should resign. He has lied to the American people, time and time again, and betrayed their trust. Since he has admitted guilt, there is no reason to put the American people through an impeachment...The only possible solution is for the president to save some dignity and resign.

Unintentional irony from 12th Congressional District candidate William Jefferson Clinton, during the Watergate controversy in 1974 (Reprinted in The Kansas City Star, *10/11/98).*

There's just no such thing as truth when it comes to him. He just says whatever sounds good and worries about it after the election.

*Candidate Bill Clinton describing his opponent, President George H. W. Bush (*The American Spectator, *10/28/92).*

I am trying to be honest with you and it hurts me.

Feeling his own pain, President Clinton during his August 17, 1998, grand jury testimony regarding the Monica Lewinsky scandal (CNN, 09/21/98).

Nobody's had a tougher press than I have. No candidate in history has.

*Bill Clinton during the 1992 campaign (*Pattern of Deception, *p. 12). Eighty-nine percent of the Washington press corps voted for Bill Clinton in that same election.*

What does that whore think she's doing to me?...[She's] a fucking slut.

*During the 1992 campaign, Bill Clinton regarding Gennifer Flowers going public with their long affair (*High Crimes & Misdemeanors, *p. 80). The ever-sensitive Hillary once said that she would "crucify" Ms. Flowers (*Hillary's Choice, *p. 13).*

That little Greek motherfucker!

Bill Clinton, angry with Michael Dukakis after the Dukakis team ridiculed his long-winded speech at the 1988 Democratic National Convention as endless and self-serving (Partners in Power, *p. 439*).

Bob Dole is not a nice man. Bob Dole is evil. The things he wants to do to children are evil. The things he wants to do to poor people and old people and sick people are evil. Let's get that straight.

President Clinton's opinion of the Senate majority leader, circa 1995 (Townhall.com, 07/06/00). Senator Dole and the evil Republicans were at the time pushing welfare reform, something that Clinton and his aides would later cite as one of the primary achievements of his presidency. After the 1996 election, Bill Clinton awarded the Presidential Medal of Freedom to the evil Bob Dole.

He couldn't get a whore across a bridge.

Bill Clinton displaying his famed sensitivity for others' pain as he discusses Ted Kennedy's "accident" at Chappaquiddick (Bill & Hillary, *p. 238*).

Ted Kennedy's car being pulled out of the water near Chappaquiddick where Mary Jo Kopechne met her untimely demise.

[Cuomo] acts like a Mafioso...[He's] a mean son of a bitch.

Bill on New York Governor Mario Cuomo, while being taped in a phone call by Gennifer Flowers during the 1992 campaign (High Crimes & Misdemeanors, *p. 47). After claiming that Flowers was lying about their affair, and that the taped phone calls were doctored, Clinton apologized to Governor Cuomo* (High Crimes & Misdemeanors, *pp. 47-48).*

The other thing we have to do is to take seriously the role of this problem of...older men who prey on underage women...There are consequences to decisions and...one way or the other, people always wind up being held accountable.

A notably straight-faced President Clinton endorsing a national effort against teen pregnancy (National Review Online, 09/18/98). *Born July 23, 1973, Monica Lewinsky was twenty-two and an intern when she started making goo-goo eyes at the then forty-nine year-old President Clinton.*

I am probably the only president who knew something about agriculture when I got here.

President Bill Clinton in a speech to farmers (St. Louis Post-Dispatch, *11/13/96). George Washington was a tobacco farmer; Thomas Jefferson was an agronomist; Jimmy "Killer Rabbit" Carter was a peanut farmer.*

The last time I checked, the Constitution said, "of the people, by the people and for the people." That's what the Declaration of Independence says.

President Bill Clinton (Seattle-Post Intelligencer, 09/20/97). *Strike Three! That statement only appears in the Gettysburg Address.*

All my life, since I was a little boy, I've heard about the Iowa caucuses.

(Drake.edu, 02/11/96). Bill Clinton has his own "Sir Edmund Hillary" moment—the Iowa caucuses began in 1972, when Clinton was avoiding the draft as a Rhodes scholar in England.

Anyone who sleeps with that bitch deserves a medal!

Bill Clinton's opinion of Sally Quinn, the wife of former Washington Post *editor Ben Bradlee* (The Survivor, *pp. 356-357). Clinton was fuming to aides as he prepared to award the Presidential Medal of Freedom to Mr. Bradlee.*

Democrat Leaders

I hate the Republicans and everything they stand for...This is a struggle between good and evil and we're the good.

Howard "The Scream" Dean (Meet the Press, *05/22/05).*

He is basically a liberal Democrat...The bottom line is that Bernie Sanders votes with the Democrats 98 percent of the time.

Howard "The Scream" Dean's opinion of Vermont Congressman Bernie Sanders, a self-admitted Socialist (Meet the Press, *05/22/05). But, Howard, is Bernie moving to the right, or is your party moving to the left?*

Uh oh, Howard's got an "evil" Republican in his sights.

The people out there who are hurt the most are the small people, and once again the wealthy special interests got to take their money off the table...

Then-DNC Chairman Terry McAuliffe on executives who sell their stock at a huge profit just before their companies declare bankruptcy (Newsmax.com, 01/31/02).

I invested in many companies, and I'm happy this one worked. This is capitalism. You invest in stock, it goes up, it goes down. You know, if you don't like capitalism, you don't like making money with stock, move to Cuba or China.

Terry McAuliffe's response to criticism after it's revealed that he invested $100,000 in Global Crossing stock and sold his shares for $18 million, shortly before the company declared bankruptcy (Newsmax.com, 01/31/02). One wonders why he didn't he just invoke the Sgt. Schultz defense?

Friends of the Black Man

I'll have them niggers voting Democrat for the next two hundred years.

Circa 1964, President Lyndon Baines Johnson's vow after he signed into law civil rights legislation (Inside the White House, p. 33).

LBJ—true civil rights champion.

[S]ome nigger, some junior high nigger kicks Steve's ass...He had the nigger down; he let him up...

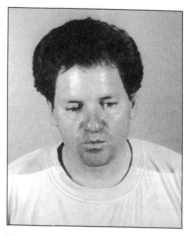

First brother and class act Roger Clinton describing an altercation, on a police surveillance video in 1984, just minutes before snorting cocaine (You Don't Say, pp. 31-32). In the same surveillance video, Roger was captured saying, "Got to get some for my brother, he's got a nose like a vacuum cleaner" (You Don't Say, p. 32). Roger Clinton is Bill Clinton's half-brother.

Roger Clinton in a police booking photo.

The Klan is needed today as never before and I am anxious to see its rebirth here in West Virginia and in every state in the Union...[I'll never fight] with a Negro by my side. Rather I should die a thousand times, and see Old Glory trampled in the dirt never to rise again, than to see this beloved land of ours become degraded by race mongrels, a throwback to the blackest specimen from the wilds.

Democrat, self-proclaimed "West Virginian for the 20th Century," and former KKK member Robert C. Byrd's letter to the Grand Wizard just a few years after he supposedly quit the group in the 1940s, cited by Michelle Malkin in her column "Senator Robert Byrd, ex-Klansman" (Townhall.com, 03/07/01). Senator Byrd also used the term "white nigger" in March 2001, describing people who are "white trash" (Fox News Sunday, 03/04/01).

The Fourth Estate

When the charge has something to do with somebody's priv would prefer not to run any of it.

Who,

Soon-to-be-disgraced Dan Rather explaining to Bill O'Reilly why he opted not to air Juanita Broaddrick's rape allegations against President Bill Clinton on The CBS Evening News *(The O'Reilly Factor, 05/15/01).*

Some sexual habits reflect an attitude toward other people, especially women, that is worth knowing about in the voting booth. It's also worth knowing if a politician is a liar and hypocrite, which he is if he's campaigning with his wife and canoodling with someone else...Denying people information they would find useful because you think they shouldn't find it useful is censorship, not journalism.

Liberal columnist Michael Kinsley chastising his readers for showing little interest in the rumors about Arnold Schwarzenegger's sex life, and the journalists who refused to write about them (WashingtonPost.com, 09/05/03).

I'm sick of talking about values, sick of pretending I have them or care more about them than I really do...When I want values, I go to Wal-Mart.

Michael Kinsley singing a somewhat different tune in the aftermath of the 2004 presidential elections, where many voters said "values" were the number one issue they voted on (The Los Angeles Times, 11/28/04).

The Feminists

[They should] stop wasting time on unprovable charges.

NOW President Patricia Ireland's response to allegations that Bill Clinton committed rape against Juanita Broaddrick in 1978 (Salon.com, 03/99).

All of us knew he was a snake when we voted for him.

Patricia Ireland, president of the National Organization of Women speaking on National Public Radio (National Public Radio, 12/09/02).

Juanita Broaddrick? I've never heard of her!

Founder of modern feminism Betty Friedan's response when asked about the woman raped by Bill Clinton (NewsMax.com, 04/12/00). The IRS has heard of Mrs. Broaddrick. In June of 2000, just over a year after going public about the rape, she became yet another critic of the Clintons to be subjected to an audit.

Other Liberals on the Clintons

There is nothing that this man won't do. He is immune to shame. Move past all the nice posturing and get really down in there on him, you find absolutely nothing...nothing but appetite.

Jesse Jackson in 1992 (National Review Online, 10/30/03).

Just because his semen is on her dress doesn't mean they had sex.

Democrat strategist Victor Kamber on Monica's infamous dress from The Gap (Fox News, 12/14/01).

Clinton's an unusually good liar. Unusually good.

Senator Bob Kerrey, D-NE (The Wall Street Journal, 08/19/98).

He was an arrogant, no-good son of a bitch...a dirty rotten scoundrel.

Editor of the Arkansas Democrat-Gazette on Bill Clinton (Spin Cycle, p. 70).

The Gap's most famous clothing item.

I quote from former U.S. Senator Paul Simon, one of my favorite Democratic colleagues, who appeared with me on a television program before the trial, who said: "You have to be an extreme Clinton zealot to believe perjury was not committed."

Senator James Inhofe, R-OK, in a closed-door impeachment statement released into the Congressional Record on February 12, 1999 (CNN.com, 02/12/99).

It is clear the president lied when he testified before the grand jury. The president has to be held to a higher standard and must be held accountable.

Representative Charles Schumer's, D-NY, statement before the Senate Judiciary Committee, found in the Democrat Judiciary section of the Congressional website (House.gov, 10/05/98). Nevertheless, four months later, as the newly elected senator from New York serving alongside Hillary, Schumer voted to acquit Bill Clinton.

Bill Clinton finally facing the music, and the nation, about lying to the grand jury.

I don't think there is any doubt that some of the factors in his pardon were attributable to his large gifts. In my opinion, that was disgraceful.

Former President Jimmy "Killer Rabbit" Carter regarding Clinton's pardon of the fugitive Marc Rich (The Washington Times, 02/22/01).

Clinton is very bright and very impressive on a first meeting. But over time I came to conclude that he was 90 percent concerned about the PR and only 10 percent substantive, at least on dealings with the CIA.

Former CIA Director James Woolsey (Why America Slept, p. 64).

Jimmy Carter, perhaps contemplating why he's been called one of the worst presidents of the 20th century.

Such behavior is not just inappropriate, it is immoral and it is harmful, for it sends a message of what is acceptable behavior to the larger American family, particularly to our children.

Senator Joe Lieberman, D-CT, on Bill Clinton's conduct in the Monica Lewinsky scandal, just four months before voting to acquit him in the impeachment trial (CNN.com, 09/03/98).

We say that from the platform of our record of consistently criticizing Mr. Clinton's ugly little lies, his abject failure to lead by example and to speak truthfully to the American people ...He is, in sum, a man you cannot trust whether you have his handshake, his signature, or his word on a Bible.

(The New York Times Editorial, 12/16/98).

The Ragin' Cajun, James Carville, doing his best imitation of Michael Corleone.

[D]efending President Clinton is like being in the Mafia, you just can't get out of the thing. I'm like Michael Corleone. How do I get out of this business?

James Carville during a debate with Bill O'Reilly in Monterey, California, circa 2001 (NewsMax.com, 01/14/02).

Hillary Rodham Clinton has already flopped as a senior administrative official in the executive branch...Perhaps she will make a good senator. But there is no reason to think that she would be anything but an abysmal president.

J. Bradford DeLong, former Clinton administration official for economic policy, recalling Hillary's attempt to pass government-run health care, quoted by David Frum (National Review Online, 06/08/03).

Hillary, though a Methodist, thinks of herself like an Episcopal bishop who deserves to live at the level of her wealthy parishioners, in return for devoting her life to God and good works.

A Clinton aide's explanation, according to Maureen "Short Irish Bitch" Dowd, as to why Hillary seeks the finer things in life while zealously crusading to deprive others of them (The New York Times, *06/29/03*).

I'm a mother-fucking tour guide for Hillary.

Clinton administration Commerce Secretary, Ron Brown complaining to his lover shortly before his death (Hell To Pay, *p. 288*). *The Clinton administration had been selling seats on Brown's foreign trade missions for $50,000 apiece, under orders from Hillary* (Hell To Pay, *pp. 287-288*).

I like Senator Clinton...she is not even vaguely the left-wing harridan portrayed by the Precambrian right. I also think that a Clinton presidential candidacy in 2008 would be a disaster on many levels. It would doubtless be a circus, a revisitation of the carnival ugliness that infested public life in the 1990s.

Primary Colors *author Joe Klein (Time.com, 05/08/05).*

She's duplicitous. She would say or do anything that would forward her ambitions. She can look you straight in the eye and lie...Lying isn't a sufficient word; it's distortion—distorting the truth to fit the case.

Liz Moynihan, wife of former New York Senator Pat Moynihan, on Hillary (The Truth About Hillary, *p. 169*).

As a lifelong active liberal Democrat, I find the choice [between Hillary and Mayor Giuliani] not difficult. In all our campaigns, we were trying to work for decent and intelligent government. Neither Clinton can give us that. It is not in their character; and their hands are too dirty.

Bartle Bull, a lawyer and writer who served as Robert F. Kennedy's New York campaign manager (The New York Post, *07/21/99*).

Everyone is fed up with the creepy dynamics of this warped marriage. We have lost all hope of getting any shred of authenticity from either Bill or Hillary...They have chosen tactics over truth with such consistency that it's impossible to accept anything they say.

Long-time Democratic apologist and columnist Maureen "Irish Bitch" Dowd (The New York Times, *08/04/99*).

The Clintons are a terminally unethical and vulgar couple, and they've betrayed everyone who has ever believed in them

Bob Herbert, another liberal writer (The New York Times, *02/26/01*).

Bill and Hillary came from Arkansas where they were always used to being the smartest people in the room. So they just naturally assumed they were the smartest people in the room in Washington, too. Anyone who had any different idea than they had was dismissed as part of...the problem.

Former Clinton administration official Donna Shalala (The Survivor, *p. 117*). *Ms. Shalala tried to warn the Clinton administration that they were pursuing the wrong strategy for health care reform. However, her objections "were dismissed as jealousy that she was not the one put in charge of the reform effort"* (The Survivor, *p. 117*).

"Grifters" was a term used in the Great Depression to describe fast-talking con artists who roamed the countryside, profiting at the expense of the poor and the uneducated, always one step ahead of the law, moving on before they were held accountable for their schemes and half-truths.

Hamilton Jordan, former White House chief of staff in the Carter administration, on why he thinks the Clintons fit the description of "grifters" to a "T" (The Wall Street Journal, *02/20/01*).

If there's one thing I've learned over the past seven years, it's how to hold my tongue.

Hillary Clinton, Circa 1999, while campaigning for Senator (Hillary's Choice, *p. 363)*

A man who could do what Clinton did in 1992 is a man whose solipsism for self-control and whose capacity for lying are so far beyond the norm of behavior as to fairly be called pathological. Hillary Rodham Clinton played the crucial, knowing role in foisting such a man upon the nation. And she did this without the slightest evident concern for what that might mean for the welfare of the nation.

Michael Kelly (Jewish World Review.com, 07/15/99)

References

Aldrich, Gary. *Unlimited Access: An FBI Agent Inside the Clinton White House.* Washington, DC: Regnery Publishing, Inc., 1996.

Andersen, Christopher, *American Evita: Hillary Clinton's Path to Power.* New York: William Morrow & Co., 2004.

_____. *Bill & Hillary: The Marriage.* New York: William Morrow & Co., 1999.

Baker, Peter. *The Breach: Inside the Impeachment and Trial of William Jefferson Clinton.* New York: Scribner, 2000.

Brock, David. *The Real Anita Hill.* New York: The Free Press, 1993.

_____. *The Seduction of Hillary Rodham.* New York: Simon & Schuster, 1996.

Brown, Kendall. *The Rants, Raves & Thoughts of Bill Clinton.* New York: On Your Own Publications, 2003.

Brown, L.D. *Crossfire: Witness in the Clinton Investigation.* Chula Vista, CA: Black Forest Press, 1999.

Califano, Joseph. *Inside: A Public and Private Life.* New York: Public Affairs, 2004.

Carpozi, George, Jr. *Clinton Confidential: The Climb to Power: The Unauthorized Biography of Bill and Hillary Clinton.* Del Mar, CA: Emery Dalton Books, 1995.

Clinton, Hillary. *It Takes a Village.* New York: Simon & Schuster, 1996.

_____. *Living History.* New York: Scribner, 2003.

Clinton, Hillary Rodham and Claire G. Osborne. *The Unique Voice of Hillary Rodham Clinton: A Portrait in Her Own Words.* New York: Avon Books, 1997.

Clinton, William Jefferson. *My Life.* New York: Knopf Publishers, 2004.

Coulter, Ann. *High Crimes & Misdemeanors: The Case Against Bill Clinton.* Washington, DC: Regnery Publishing, Inc., 1998.

_____. *Slander: Liberal Lies About the American Right.* New York: Crown Publishers, 2002.

Elder, Larry. *Showdown: Confronting Bias, Lies, and the Special Interests that Divide America*. New York: St. Martin's Press, 2002.

Gergen, David. *Eyewitness to Power: The Essence of Leadership Nixon to Clinton* New York: Simon & Schuster, 2000.

Gielow, Fred. *You Don't Say: Sometimes Liberals Show Their True Colors*. Boca Raton, FL: Freedom Books, 1999.

Graham, Tim. *Pattern of Deception: The Media's Role in the Clinton Presidency*. Washington, DC: Media Research Center, 1996.

Gross, Martin L. *The Great Whitewater Fiasco*. New York: Ballantine Books, 1994.

Hannity, Sean. *Let Freedom Ring: Winning the War of Liberty Over Liberalism*. New York: Harper Collins, 2002.

Harris, John F. *The Survivor: Bill Clinton in the White House*. New York: Random House, 2005.

Hastert, Dennis. *Speaker: Lessons from Forty Years in Coaching and Politics*. Washington, DC: Regnery Publishing, Inc., 2004

Hayward, Stephen. *The Real Jimmy Carter: How Our Worst Ex-President Undermines American Foreign Policy, Coddles Dictators, and Created the Party of Clinton and Kerry*. Washington, DC: Regnery Publishing, Inc., 2004.

Hubbell, Webb. *Friends in High Places: Our Journey From Little Rock to Washington, D.C.* New York: William Morrow & Co., 1997.

Ingraham, Laura. *The Hillary Trap: Looking for Power in All the Wrong Places*. New York: Hyperion, 2000.

Isikoff, Michael. *Uncovering Clinton: A Reporter's Story*. New York: Crown Publishers, 1999.

Kessler, Ronald. *A Matter of Character: Inside the White House of George W. Bush*. New York: Sentinel Books, 2004.

_____. *Inside the White House*. New York: Pocket, 1996.

Klein, Ed. *The Truth About Hillary: What She Knew, When She Knew It, and How Far She'll Go to Become President*. New York: Sentinel, 2005.

Kurtz, Howard. *Spin Cyle: How the White House and the Media Manipulate the News*. New York: Free Press, 1998.

Limbacher, Carl. *Hillary's Scheme: Inside the Next Clinton's Ruthless Agenda to Take the White House.* New York: Crown Forum, 2003.

Limbaugh, David. *Absolute Power: The Legacy of Corruption in the Clinton-Reno Justice Department.* Washington, DC. Regnery Publishing, Inc., 2001.

Lowry, Rich. *Legacy: Paying The Price for the Clinton Years.* Washington, DC: Regnery Publishing, Inc., 2003.

Maraniss, David. *First in His Class: A Biography of Bill Clinton.* New York: Simon & Schuster, 1995.

Matalin, Mary and James Carville. *All's Fair: Love, War, and Running For President.* New York: Random House, 1994.

McDougal, Jim and Curtis Wilkie. *Arkansas Mischief: The Birth of a National Scandal.* New York: Henry Holt & Company, 1998.

Medved, Michael. *Right Turns: Unconventional Lessons from a Controversial Life.* New York: Crown Forum Publishers: 2004

Milton, Joyce. *The First Partner: Hillary Rodham Clinton.* New York: William Morrow & Co., 1999.

Morris, Dick. *Rewriting History.* New York: Regan Books, 2004.

Morris, Roger. *Partners in Power: The Clintons and Their America.* New York: Henry Holt & Company, 1996.

Noonan, Peggy. *The Case Against Hillary Clinton.* New York: Regan Books, 2000.

Oakley, Meredith. *On the Make: The Rise of Bill Clinton.* Washington, DC: Regnery Publishing, Inc., 1994.

Olson, Barbara. *Hell to Pay: The Unfolding Story of Hillary Rodham Clinton.* Washington, DC: Regnery Publishing, Inc., 1999.

_____. *The Final Days: The Last, Desperate Abuses of Power by the Clinton White House.* Washington, DC: Regnery Publishing, Inc., 2001.

Oppenheimer, Jerry. *The State of a Union: Inside the Complex Marriage of Bill and Hillary Clinton.* New York: Harper Collins Publishing, 2000.

O'Reilly, Bill. *The No Spin Zone: Confrontations With the Powerful and Famous in America.* New York: Broadway Books, 2001.

Patterson, Lt. Col. Robert "Buzz." *Dereliction of Duty: The Eyewitness Account of How Bill Clinton Endangered America's Long-Term National Security.* Washington, DC: Regnery Publishing, Inc., 2003.

_____. *Reckless Disregard: How Liberal Democrats Undercut Our Military, Endanger Our Soldiers, and Jeopardize Our Security.* Washington, DC: Regnery Publishing Inc., 2004.

Posner, Gerald L. *Why America Slept: The Failure to Prevent 9/11.* New York: Random House, 2003.

Rodcliffe, Donnie. *Hillary Rodham Clinton: A First Lady for Our Time.* New York: Warner Books, 1993.

Ruddy, Christopher and Carl Limbacher, Jr., eds., *Bitter Legacy: Newsmax.com Reveals the Untold Story of the Clinton-Gore Years.* West Palm Beach, FL: NewsMaxMedia, 2001.

_____. *Hillary Clinton's Plans for the Presidency: Know The Real Hillary! The Story The Media Won't Report.* NewsMax.com, 2001.

Sheehy, Gail. *Hillary's Choice.* New York: Ballantine Publishing Group, 1999.

Stephanopoulos, George. *All Too Human.* New York: Little Brown & Co., 1999.

Stewart, James. *Blood Sport: The Truth Behind the Scandals in the Clinton White House.* New York: Simon & Schuster, 1996.

Toobin, Jeffrey. *A Vast Conspiracy: The Real Story of the Sex Scandal that Nearly Brought Down a President.* New York: Random House, 1999.

Tyrell, R. Emmett. *Boy Clinton: A Political Biography.* Washington, DC: Regnery Publishing, Inc., 1996.

_____. *Madame Hillary: The Dark Road to the White House.* Washington, DC: Regnery Publishing, Inc., 2004.

Woodward, Bob. *Shadow: Five Presidents and the Legacy of Watergate.* New York: Simon & Schuster, 1999.

_____. *The Agenda: Inside the Clinton White House.* New York: Simon & Schuster, 1994.

_____. *The Choice*: November 5, 1996. New York: Simon & Schuster, 1996

For the Best Conservative Books, Look for

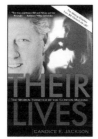
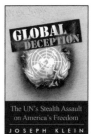

Tom Kuiper

Thomas D. Kuiper is a paralegal for a large California corporation. Tom was born in Iowa and graduated from Iowa State University with a degree in communications. He's worked on several projects for the conservative website Newsmax, and was the researcher behind the enormously popular "Deck of Hillary" playing cards, the site's most successful product ever. Tom lives in the San Francisco Bay area.

Dick Morris & Eileen McGann

Dick Morris served as Bill Clinton's political consultant for twenty years, guiding him to a successful reelection in 1996. He now appears on Fox News and has served as a consultant for foreign leaders, including President Vincente Fox of Mexico. He is the author of the *New York Times* bestsellers *Condi vs. Hillary*, *Because He Could*, *Rewriting History* (both with Eileen McGann), *Off with Their Heads*, and *Behind the Oval Office*.